Barbara T. Smith

I Am Abandoned

Barbara T. Smith

I Am Abandoned

Performed in collaboration
with Richard Rubinstein

Primary Information

Contents

Artist Statement

I decided to seek authority in the male world. Thinking I knew the language, had truly novel and valid ideas, and could speak the tongue, I would seek to validate myself and through me, other women. I had the idea, checked out its novelty, and ran pell-mell to present it.

I had been invited by David Smith at the Baxter Art Gallery at Caltech to participate in a show that would be called *The Many Arts of Science*. Dick Rubinstein and I had been discussing a collaboration and since he was a Caltech graduate, he had the necessary connections.

What interested me was this goofy program called DOCTOR, which was a serious project created by Joseph Weizenbaum. DOCTOR was a Rogerian therapist program whereby the user could enquire of the therapist about their mental health and, on a basic level, be "treated." I also knew through Dick of another paranoid schizophrenic program called PARRY, which exhibited four levels of disturbance. We fantasized about linking the two programs.

The difficulty was that Dick would be in Boston when the show happened, but that only made it more interesting. He would make the connection at a distance.

For me, the piece needed to be fleshed out with more meaning, a feminist perspective. It all resonated with my experience and my extreme current dilemma. Men seemed, unlike women at the time, to be more fascinated with their toys, their careers, their hobbies, and sports than with quality time with their mates. Men seemed to have wives to take care of the shit work, the nest, the correspondence, and to be there when needed for a good fuck, but wives were not the focus of their world. For women, the relationship was paramount. It was the source of her joy, replenishment of her energy, and the grounding and inspirational match for her own endeavors. It was a built-in problem, and these computers were only a new example.

I needed to get good slides of Goya's *Duchess of Alba*, naked and clothed. To my surprise, the Los Angeles County Museum did not have any, nor did the Metropolitan in New York. I was told I had to either photograph a textbook or write the museum in Spain that owns the works. I phoned and they sent me two 4 × 5" slides of exquisite quality, but with serious restrictions on their use.

It was illegal to copy them and whatever I did was going to cost me more money than I had. I phoned to say there had been a misunderstanding and I would be sending them back by return mail. In the meantime, I shot two images of my hand holding each slide aloft and due to the size of the image they are quite clear. The plan had been to get my student Kathy Niles to recline on a chaise lounge as per one of the images and to project the other over her.

On the day of the piece, Dick's friend John Vital set up the terminals in the gallery. I had hoped to have the entire arrangement in one place, but we ended up needing to install the terminal in one small area and position Kathy in a nearby room. In the room with the terminal, we also set up an overhead projector where we could project the readouts from the dialogue.

John, myself, and others did indeed first talk to DOCTOR. Then we connected with Dick in Boston. For my part, I tried to get DOCTOR to think. I wanted the program to integrate information I gave it and come to an independent conclusion. Of course, a futile idea. Finally, we/they connected the two programs.

In the meantime, John at Caltech and Dick at MIT had to be totally engrossed in the game, while Kathy, who looked beautiful on the chaise, was fuming. She chewed her bubble gum and waited for attention as illogical conversations were sequentially projected on the wall to be read by all. Finally in a fury she got off the divan and stormed into the room where the computer and John sat with a small crowd around him. She sidled up to him, sat on his lap, and tried to seduce him.

It is a very funny piece, but I think it upset David Smith. He didn't like that it was taking attention away from the more static pieces and installations and he suddenly told me he wanted the piece shut down. I was appalled and refused. He then shut down the power. It was embarrassing and confusing to me, and I did not know what was wrong. I suppose now we had not clearly communicated what would actually happen. I expected more help and understanding from him, and he expected the same from me. I was furious, and apparently, he was too. It took a few years before we spoke again. Happily, our paths rarely crossed anyway.

NON-PROFIT ORG.
U S POSTAGE
P A I D
PASADENA, CALIF.
PERMIT 583

CALIFORNIA INSTITUTE OF TECHNOLOGY
BAXTER ART GALLERY
PASADENA, CA 91125

Baxter Art Gallery

CALIFORNIA INSTITUTE OF TECHNOLOGY

THE MANY ARTS OF SCIENCE

MUSIC, POETRY, AND THE VISUAL ARTS FROM
BELL LABS, CAL COMP, CALTECH, CRANBROOK

ANAIT
CHOWNING
COORS
DEMOS
HOWLETT
KOWALSKI
LINTAULT
MALLORY
SCHARFF
SMITH
SQUIRES
STABROWSKI
TINGUELY
WHITNEY
B. ZIMMERMAN
E. ZIMMERMAN

COMPUTER AND MACHINE GENERATED ART
HOLOGRAMS AND OTHER OPTICAL EFFECTS

BAXTER ART GALLERY
CALIFCRNIA INSTITUTE OF TECHNOLOGY

FEBRUARY 19 THRU MARCH 13, 1976
NOON TO 5 CAILY EXCEPT MONDAY

YOU ARE CORDIALLY INVITED TO THE OPENING
ON FEBRUARY 19, FROM 7 TO 10

JOHN CHOWNING WILL PLAY AND EXPLAIN HIS
MUSIC. JOHN WHITNEY WILL SHOW HIS FILMS

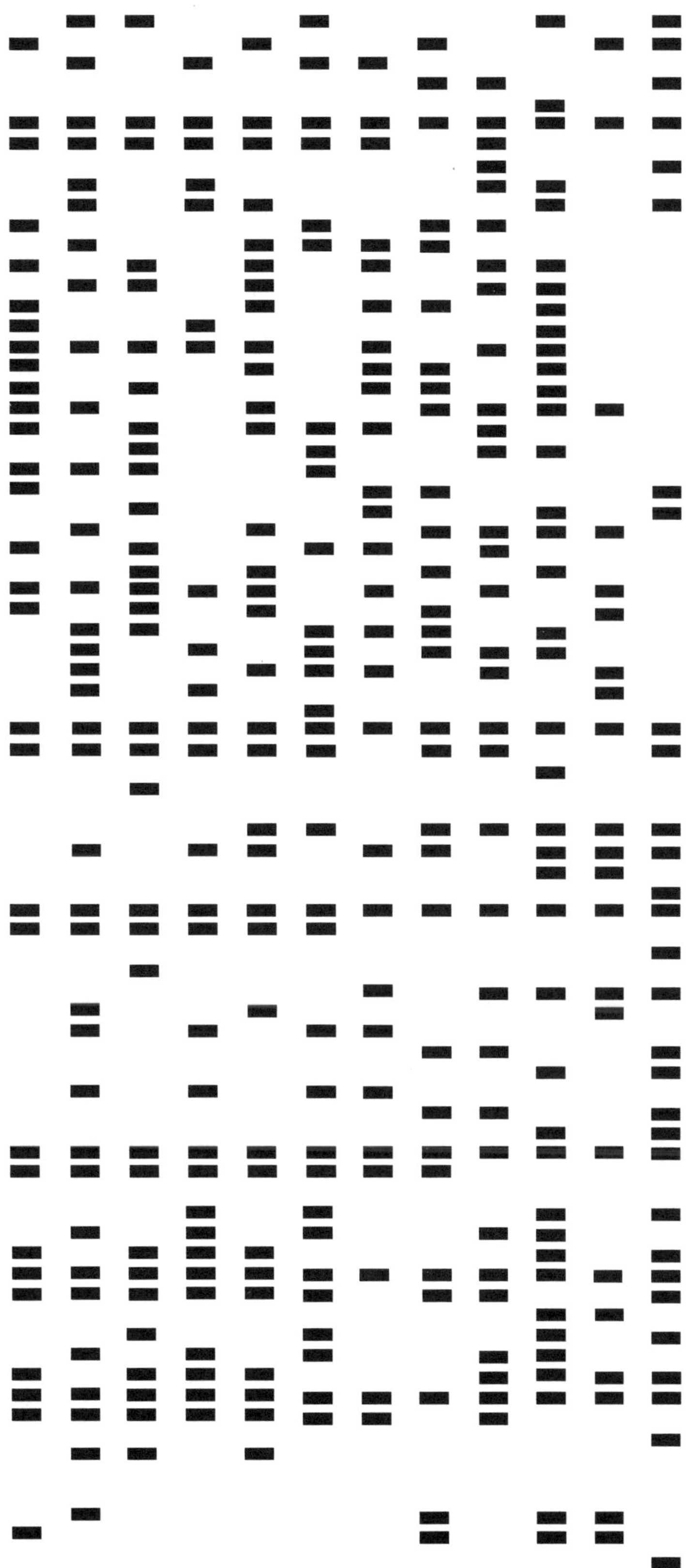

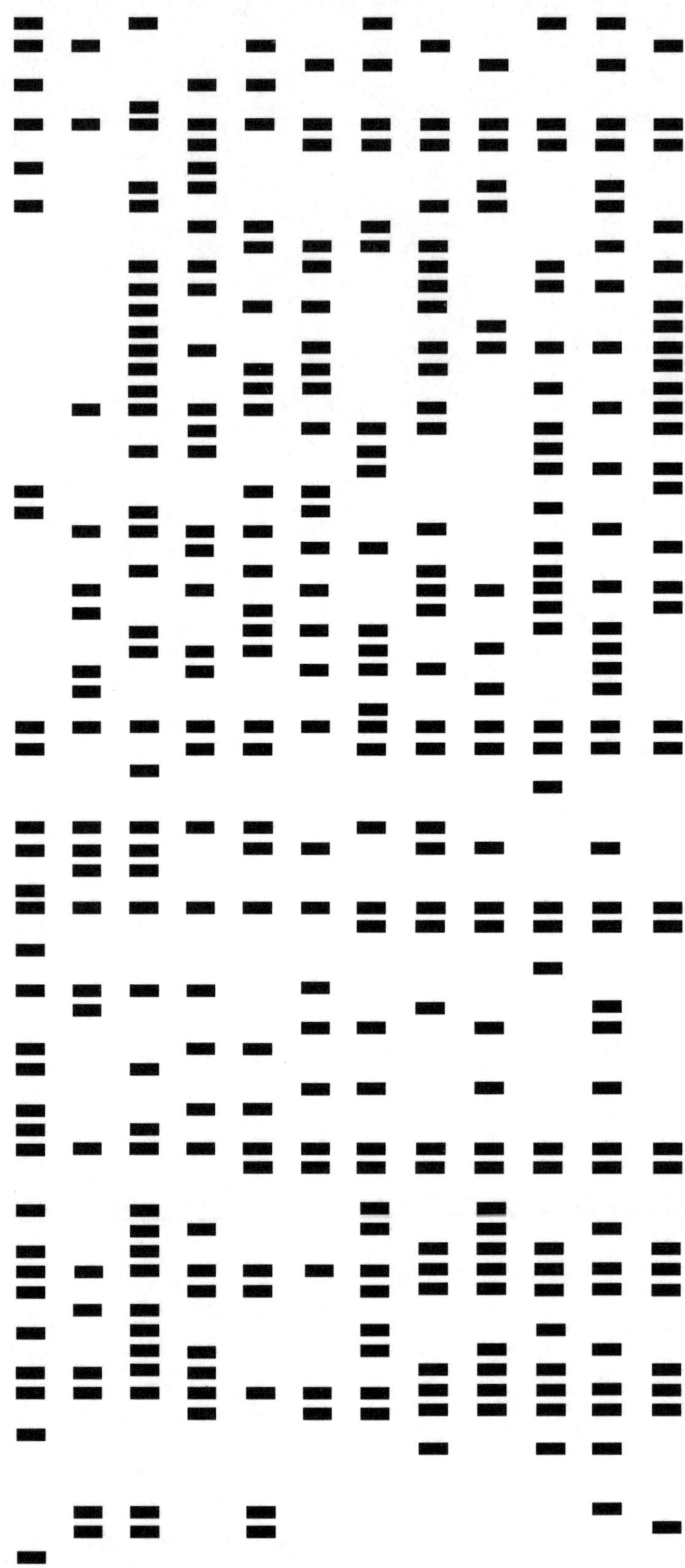

```
@
@netstAt.SAV;2

*h
*dECIMAL.HOST.NUMBERS
*


THE FOLLOWING ARE UP:

 65. UCLA-CCN        143. I4B-TENEX      228. HAWAII-500
 66. SRI-AI           16. AMES-67         42. LONDON
  4. UTAH-10          18. RADC-MULTICS   106. LONDON-VDH
197. BBN-TENEXA       19. NBS-10          43. OFFICE-1
  6. MIT-DEVMULTICS   21. LLL-RISOS       44. MIT-MULTICS
 70. MIT-DMS          86. USC-ISI        236. 354
134. MIT-AI          150. USC-ISIC        46. RUTGERS-10
198. MIT-ML          214. USC-ISID        49. BBN-TENEXB
  7. RAND-RCC         23. USC-44         241. BBN-TENEX
  8. SDC-LAB         215. USC-ECL        114. BBN-TENEXD
  9. HARV-10          28. ARPA-DMS       244. USC-ISIB
 10. LL               31. CCA-TENEX       55. ANL
 11. SU-AI            32. PARC-MAXC       56. SUMEX-AIM
 14. CMU-10B          34. LBL            191. 277
 78. CMU-10A^C
@XXX
@det
 DETACHING JOB # 47
@c
 Closed
@o 114
Trying...
 Host broke the connection
@o 114
Trying...
 Open
```

```
@c
 Closed T
@o 1 Can't
@o 1 Can't
@r


ISI TIP 350 #: 17
@o 114
Trying...
 Open

 BBN-TENEX 1.34.2, BBN-SYSTEM-D EXEC 1.54.2
@WH RUBIN
 NOT LOGGED IN
@WH RUBINSTEIN
 TTY22, JOB 12, 191, LISP
 DETACHED, JOB 27  LISP
 DETACHED, JOB 28  (PRIV)
@LOG RUBINSTEIN
 ?
@
@LOG RUG/GBINSEIN  ?

@OPHIEXXX
@LOG RUBINSTEIN
 ?
@LINK
        ?
@LINK (TO) ? ONE OF THE FOLLOWING:
TERMINAL NUMBER
USER NAME
 LINK (TO) RUBINSTEIN
LINK FROM , JOB 25, TTY 26
7
@
```

```
@LOGO 28
@;WHATS YOUR APASSWORD.  JJV HERE
@;TODAY, IT'S ART !
@LOG RUBINSTEIN
(ACCOUNT #)
 JOB 25 ON TTY26 19-FEB-76 21:27
 PREVIOUS LOGIN: 19-FEB-76 21:20
 [JOB 12 ALSO LOGGED IN UNDER RUBINSTEIN]

 [RUBINSTEIN OVER ALLOCATION BY 1992 PAGES]
@;YOU STILL THERE?
@;YUP.  HOW'RE THINGS?
@;HEADACDHIE.
@
@;THAT'S TOO BAD.  ARE THINGS SET UP? DOES BARBARA WANT TO TRY OUT ANYT
**HING?
@;WELL, I'M HERE, THE TERMINAL IS HERE, WE'RE TALKING TO YOU.
@;WHAT MORE COULD WE ASK FOR?
@
@;no comment. We When you do the run, would you do it thru TELNET
@;so that we get a copy.  You might go thru ISI if that seems OK...
@
@;NO -- NET DELAYS TOO MUCH.  MAYBE THRU THERE. OK?
@;fine. Lets be sure to copy the file before anyone logs off, though.
@
@;OK -- HERE GOES.
@
@NO RAI
@tel
 ?
@;John  I'm going to break for the moment.  Do you need me for a little
** while?
@;don't know.  B. is not here right now.
@
@;ok.  Please link to me a little later.  I'm on the brun brink (but ju
**st) of getting the Parry / doctor thing to work...
```

```
@;ok -- cul..
@br
@
@telnet

User Telnet 3.5 14-Jun-74.  Type HELP<cr> for help.
*bbnd is complete.#

 BBN-TENEX 1.34.2, BBN-SYSTEM-D EXEC 1.54.2
@LOG RUBINSTEIN
(ACCOUNT #)
 JOB 28 ON TTY27 19-FEB-76 21:32
 PREVIOUS LOGIN: 19-FEB-76 21:27
 [JOBS 12, 25 ALSO LOGGED IN UNDER RUBINSTEIN]

 [RUBINSTEIN OVER ALLOCATION BY 1992 PAGES]
@

@NO RAI
@
#transparent.mode #
no
#no transparent.mode #
 ?
@
@
#?
connection.to
disconnect
status.of
news
echo.mode.is
terminal.type.is
local.mode
remote.mode
no
```

current.modes.are
character.mode
line.buffer
raise
lower
transparent.mode
case.shift.prefix.for
unshift.prefix:
quote.prefix:
synch.character:
attention.character:
concise
verbose
fancy.command.interpret
divert.output.stream.to.file
typescript.to.file
signal.waiting.output
escape.character=
clear.output.character=
help
netstatus
socket.map
run
quit
logout
reset
ddt
exec
code
<octal digitsits>
d<decimal digit><any number of decimal digits>
control
!break!
!synch!
write.modes.for.host
name.current.connection.to.be

```
retrieve.connection.under.name
wait.for.any.active.connection
where.am.I
list.connections
flush.host
;<any number of any characters>
```

BBNE
AIM
ARGONNE
ISIB
BBND
BBN
BBNB
SCI
MULTICS
NIC
PARC
CCA
ECL
ISID
ISIC
ISIA
ISI
NBS
I4B
I4A
I4
CMUA
CMUB
SAIL
ACL
SDC
MATHLAB
DMS
BBNA

UTAH
UCSB
AIC
SRI-AIC
ARC
CCN
SUMEX-AIM
ANL
USC-ISIB
BBN-TENEXD
BBN-TENEX
BBN-TENEXB
RUTGERS-10
MOFFETT-ARC
MIT-MC
MIT-MULTICS
OFFICE-1
LONDON-VDH
LONDON
SDAC-44
HAWAII-500
UCSD-CC
PARC-MAXC
CCA-TENEX
ARPA-DMS
USC-ECL
USC-44
USC-ISID
USC-ISIC
USC-ISI
LLL-RISOS
NBS-10
RADC-MULTICS
AMES-67
I4B-TENEX
I4-ELF

```
I4-TENEX
CMU-10A
CMU-10B
SU-AI
LL
HARV-10
SDC-CC
SDC-LAB
RAND-ISD
RAND-RCC
MIT-ML
MIT-AI
MIT-DMS
BBN-TENEXA
UTAH-10
CHII
UCSB-MOD75
SRI-AI
UCLA-CCN
  #

#
#typescript.to.file art.transcript;1 [New file]
#

@
@jo
 TSS JOB 28, USER RUBINSTEIN, TTY27
@wh rubinstEIN
 TTY22, JOB 12, 191, LISP
 TTY31, JOB 14, BBN-TENEXD, (PRIV)
 TTY26, JOB 25, ISI-TIP, TELNET
 TTY30, JOB 27, BBN-TENEXD, LISP
 TTY27, JOB 28, BBN-TENEXD, EXEC
@dir di\ioctOR.*;*
```

<RUBINSTEIN>

DOCTOR.SAV;1

@doctor

DOCTOR 12-APR-75 ...

Hello.

TELL ME YOUR PROBLEMS. PLEASE TERMINATE INPUT WITH A PERIOD OR A RUNNIN
**G
QUESTION AT 14603 MARK.
LOAD AV. = 3.88, USED 0:06.2 IN 5:10

*HI, ARE YOU ALL RIGHT TONITE?

WHY ARE YOU INTERESTED IN WHETHER I AM ALL RIGHT TONITE OR NOT?

*
I'M NOT, BUT YOU SHOULD BE.

SUPPOSE YOU SHOULD BE.

*
BUT, I DON'T WANT TO BE
.

DON'T YOU REALLY WANT TO BE?

*
HOW REDUNDANT CAN YOU GET?

WHY DO YOU ASK?

*
YOU ASKED ME.
WHY DO YOU THINK I ASKED YOU?

*
YOU DIDN'?

OH? I DIDN'?

*
NOPE.

I AM NOT SURE I UNDERSTAND YOU FULLY.

*
THAT'S NOT UNUSUAL.

PLEASE GO ON.

*
TOMORROW.

WHAT DOES THAT SUGGEST TO YOU?

*
THAT YOU ARE DRUNK.

WHAT MAKES YOU THINK I AM DRUNK?

*
YOU ARE SLURRING YOUR WORDS.

DOES IT PLEASE YOU TO BELIEVE I AM SLURRING MY WORDS?

*
YES.

IS THERE SOMETHING BOTHERING YOU?

*
ONLY ON ODD ALTERNATE THURSDAY EVENIONGS.

WHAT ELSE WOULD YOU LIKE TO DISCUSS?

*
NOTHING.

WHY DO YOU SAY THAT JUST NOW?

*
YOU ASKED.

WHAT MAKES YOU THINK I ASKED?

*
YO MEAN YOU DIDN'T?

WHO ARE YOU REALLY TALKING ABOUT?

*
MY BEST OR WAS IT WORST FRIEND.

IS IT IMPORTANT TO YOU THAT YOUR BEST OR WAS IT WORST FRIEND?

*
DO YOU HAVE A VOCABULARY OF NOUNS?

SUPPOSE YOU HAVE A VOCABULARY OF NOUNS.

*
I KNOW I DO, BUT DO YOU?

I AM NOT SURE I UNDERSTAND YOU FULLY.

```
*
DO YOU KNOW ABOUT HORSES?

WHY DOES THAT QUESTION INTEREST YOU?

*
THEY NEIGH.

PLEASE GO ON.

*
NOT NO, THANK YOU.

LETS DISCUSS FURTHER WHY YOUR BEST OR WAS IT WORST FRIEND.

*
?<wP\P\LFY{${7s=?

WHAT DOES THAT SUGGEST TO YOU?

*K\K\U$$}G^\"$^C
@RES
@WH RUBINSTEIN
 TTY22, JOB 12, 191, LISP
 TTY31, JOB 14, BBN-TENEXD, (PRIV)
 TTY26, JOB 25, ISI-TIP, TELNET
 TTY30, JOB 27, BBN-TENEXD, LISP
 TTY27, JOB 28, BBN-TENEXD, EXEC
@CONT
 NO PROGRAM
@DOCTOR

DOCTOR  12-APR-75 ...

Good evening.
```

TELL ME YOUR PROBLEMS. PLEASE TERMINATE INPUT WITH A PERIOD OR A QUESTION MARK.

*IREALLY HAVE NO CPROBLEMS RIGHT NOW.

IS THERE SOMETHING BOTHERING YOU?

*NOT REALLY , IWANT TON DANCE WITH YOU.

I AM NOT SURE I UNDERSTAND YOU FULLY.

*YOU ALWAYS SAYTHE SAME THINGS BACK , IITHINK YOU ARE VERY DULL.

IN WHAT WAY?

*YOU HAVE NO CONVERSATION.

SUPPOSE YOU HAVE NO CONVERSATION.

*I SAID YOU HAVE NO CONVERSATION.

OH? I HAVE NO CONVERSATION?

* TYES YOU ARE EVASIVE , I THINK YOU ARE SICK.

WHAT MAKES YOU THINK I AM SICK?

*THAT WHICH I JUST SAID.

PLEASE GO ON.

*ASND ON AND ONR AND ON ANOON.

WHAT DOES THAT SUGGEST TO YOU?
*YOPU AND I WILL NEVER DANCE OR TALK OR FUCK.

WHAT ELSE WOULD YOU LIKE TO DISCUSS?

*GET LOST.

WHY DO YOU SAY THAT JUST NOW?

*I AM ANGRY.

IS IT BECAUSE YOU ARE ANGRY THAT YOU CAME TO ME?

*NBO.

ARE YOU STILL ANGRY?

*SOMEWHAT.

I AM NOT SURE I UNDERSTAND YOU FULLY.

```
*^C
@^C
@
@LINK RUBINSTEIN
 TTY27, EXEC
 TTY23, LISP
 TTY26, TELNET
 TTY25, (PRIV)
 TTY22, LISP
 TTY:   22

LINK FROM RUBINSTEIN, JOB 28, TTY 27
@;EWE'RE HERE AND READY TO GO.
@;
@ EXEC
SUBSYS - BAD FILE/FORK
131074
(ERROR broken)
```

```
9:^

 BBN-TENEX 1.34.2, BBN-SYSTEM-D EXEC 1.54.2
@;OK.  THE P/D PROGRAM LIMPS AND IS NOT YET QUITE SATISFACTORY.  BUT IT
**IS INTERESTING...  YOU ARE READY TO START NOW WITH THE PERFORMANCE?
@
@;LET'S DO THE FOLLOWING:  1. PLAY WITH DOCTOR ALONE FOR A WHILE,
@THEN ?
@. ?
@ ;THEN 2. SWITCH TO PARRY.  THESE WE CAN DO WITHOUT YOU, RIGHT?
@;THEN, AROUND 9:00 OR SO WE PITCH THEM TOGETHER.  WHATCHA THINK?
@;FIN
E

@. I'LL WAT
   CH FROM THIS END, AND MAYBE COMMENT.  I WANT T.XXX
@;SCRATCH THE\EAT.  GO AHEAD!
@
@;OK THE MASSES JUST STARTED COMING IN THE DOOR. BREAK WHEN YOU GET TIR
**ED. OK?
@
@


 ;
@



 OK



@
```

```
@;OOPS, HERE'S BARB...
@
@;HI,THE PEOPLE ARE COMING IN AND MY PEOPLE FROM JOHNSTON ARE NOT HERE Y
**ET.
@DICK/?
@;DO YOU WANT TO WAIT A FEW MINUTES, OR GO AHEAD?
@
@; IWNR TO WAIT A FEW MINIUTES>  ISN"T THIS FUN?
@
@;YES ISN'T IT!  (YOU NEED TO HIT RETURN WHEN DONE TYPEING...)
@:OOPS! I AM GLAD YOU COULD FAKE IT >
@;THE DOCTOR/PARRY PROGRAM IS LIMPING ALONG, BUT MAY BE WORTH LOOKING AT
** A LITTLE LATER.  AS IT STANDS, IT'S VERY FUNNY, BUT NOT QUITE RIGHT..
**.
@
@: ?
@ SI] ?
@?
COMMANDS ARE:
 ACCESS
 ACCOUNT
 ADVISE
 APPEND
 ARCHIVE
 ASSIGN
 ATTACH
 AVAILABLE
 BDDT
 BREAK
 CHANGE
 CLEAR
 CONNECT
 CONTINUE
 COPY
 DAYTIME
 DDT
```

```
 DEASSIGN
 DELETE
 DETACH
 DIRECTORY
 DISCUSE
 DSKSTAT
 EDIT
 ENTRY
 EPHEMERAL
 EXEC
 EXPUNGE
 FILSTAT
 FORK
 FORMFEED
 FULLDUPLEX
 GET
 GOTO
 HA INTERROGATE
 JFNCLOSE
 JOBSTAT
 LENGTH
 LINK
 LIST
 LOGIN
 LOGOUT
 LOWERCASE
 MAIL
 MEMSTAT
 M^C
@^C
@^C
@CCCC^C
@^C
@^C
@^C
@^C
```

```
@: ?
@THANK: ?
@
@: ?
@THANK  ?
@D;; ?
@;BARB-- YOU YOU HAVE TO TYPE A SIMI-COLON AT THE BEGINNING OF A LINEXXX
@
@;WHICH YOU DO NOT WANT THE COMPUTER TO INTERPRET AS A COMMAND...
@
@;I MADE A SERIOUSD MISTAKE , THANK GOD JOHN WAS HERE OR THE DAMN THING
**WOULD NEVER HAVE STOPPED.
@;NOT ALL THAT SERIOUS. IT HAD GOTTEN TO THE U'S &
  WOULD HAVE STOPPED SOON...
@;WELL DICK,I AM GOING TO REST A MINUTE SO THAT WHEN A FEW MORE PEOPLE C
**OME IN I CAN BEF/BEGIN THE PIECE.
@;GOOD.  TALK TO YOU LATER.  PLEASE PUT JOHN BACK ON.
@
@;JONH-- I'M GOING TO BREAK AND COME BACK IN A FEW MINUTES...PLEASE LINK
** TO ME WHEN YOU'RE READY TO START IF I DONT LINK FIRST...
@
@;WELL, LET'S START SOME DOCTORING RIGHT NOW.
@
@;OK, GO AHEAD.  I'LL WATCH, BUT WORK ON ANOTHER TERMINAL...
@;OK.
@
@
@
```

DOCTOR

DOCTOR 12-APR-75 ...

```
Hello.

TELL ME YOUR PROBLEMS. PLEASE TERMINATE INPUT WITH A PERIOD OR A
QUESTION MARK.

*;RR:  HAVE TO DO A COUPLE THINGS TO CLEAN UP.  JUST BE A MOMENT...
@CONT
NO PROGRAM
@QUIT

131074
87*
87*

9_CLOSEALL()
(NET:<RUBINSTEIN>5.BBND-30324200030;T
NET:<RUBINSTEIN>4.BBND-30324200031;T
NET:<RUBINSTEIN>5.BBND-30324200026;T
NET:<RUBINSTEIN>4.BBND-30324200027;T)
10_^C
@RESET
@;RESET...  THERE, THAT'S BETTER..... (RR)
@JOB:
 TSS JOB 12, USER RUBINSTEIN, TTY22
@

^C
@;WE'RE BACK WATCH AWAY.
@
@
@DOCTOR


DOCTOR 12-APR-75 ...

Hi.
```

TELL ME YOUR PROBLEMS. PLEASE TERMINATE INPUT WITH A PERIOD OR A QUESTION MARK.

*IHAAVE A O/ AN OBJECT NTHAT I AM NO T SURE OF.

IS IT BECAUSE YOU ARE NO T SURE OF THAT YOU CAME TO ME?

*YES.

IS THERE SOMETHING BOTHERING YOU?

*YES, I WANT YOU TO TE;L; ME WHAT IT IS.

SUPPOSE YOU WHAT IT WERE NOT.

*WHAT?

WHY DO YOU ASK?

*BECDAUSE I CASNNOT UNDERSTAND YOU.

I AM NOT SURE I UNDERSTAND YOU FULLY.

*OK THIS OBJECT IS RED AND IT IS WHITISH INSIDE.

POSSIBLY OK THIS OBJECT REALLY IS NOT RED AND IT IS WHITISH INSIDE.

*L.

PLEASE GO ON.

*IT WEIGHAS 62/L00 #

*.

ARE YOU STILL NO T SURE OF?

* YES.

WHY ARE YOU SO SURE?

* BECAUSRE IT A;SOPHAS OTHER PROBPERTIES.

WHAT DOES THAT SUGGEST TO YOU?

* IT IT IS COMPLESX AND THUS MAY NOT BE AN OBJECT AT ALL.

TELL ME MORE ABOUT IT IT.

*OK IT HAS 75 CALORIES.

WHAT ELSE WOULD YOU LIKE TO DISCUSS?

*MORE ABOUT IT , IT IS ALO////ALSO ON A PIECE OF PAPER AS A SYBOL.

DID YOU THINK IT MIGHT NOT BE ALO////ALSO ON A PIECE OF PAPER AS A SYBOL ?

* I MEAN SYMBOL AND I HAVE OFTEN SEEN IT SO BUTWHY IS ONE THING SO MANY?

YOU MEAN SYMBOL AND YOU HAVE OFTEN SEEN IT SO BUTWHY PERHAPS IS ONE THING SO MANY.

*.

WHY DO YOU SAY THAT JUST NOW?

*.

I AM NOT SURE I UNDERSTAND YOU FULLY.

*.

PLEASE GO ON.

*YES.

I SEE.

*DO U/ YOU SPEAK A CODE REGARDLESS OF WHAT I SAY?

SUPPOSE YOU SPEAK A CODE REGARDLESS OF WHAT YOU SAY.

*THIS OBJECT IS ALSO IN FOUR PIECES AND LATER IT WAS EATEN, IT IS NOW IN **SIDE FOUR DIFFERENT PEOPLE.

SUPPOSE THIS OBJECT WERE NOT ALSO IN FOUR PIECES AND LATER IT WAS EATEN.

*IT WOULD BE EASIER TO TELL WHAT IT IS.

POSSIBLY IT WOULD BE EASIER TO TELL WHAT IT REALLY IS NOT.

*THAT IS A VERY ASTUTE REPLY , YOU ARE VERY SMART.

WHAT MAKES YOU THINK I AM VERY SMART?

*I LOVE THE STYLE AND VERVE OF YOUR CONVERSATION.

WHAT ELSE DO YOU LOVE?

*OH THE VERY THING I AM R/ TRYING TO FING OUT ISIF YOU CAN IDENTIFY FOR **ME.

HOW LONG HAVE YOU BEEN R/ TRYING TO FING OUT ISIF I CAN IDENTIFY FOR YOU ?

*ABOUTL/15 MINUTES.

WHAT DOES THAT SUGGEST TO YOU?

*THIS IS A DIFFICULT PROBLEM BECAUSE YOU CANNOT SEE WHAT I AM DESCRIBING
** AND YOU ARE ONLY A MACHINE, (I DO NOT MENA TO HURT YOUR FEELO/INGS BY
** SAYING SO).

EARLIER YOU SAID YOU WERE R/ TRYING TO FING OUT ISIF I CAN IDENTIFY FOR YOU.

*RIGHT , CAN YOU IDENTIFY WHAT I AM TRYING TO DESCRIBE.

YOU BELIEVE I CAN IDENTIFY WHAT YOU ARE TRYING TO DESCRIBE DON'T YOU?

*?

MAYBE NOW WE CAN DISCUSS WHY YOU ARE TRYING TO DESCRIBE.

*BECAUSE IT IS NOT EASY TO FIND A TRUE OBJECT ANYMORE.

IS THAT THE REAL REASON?

*NO.

CAN YOU BE MORE INFORMATIVE?
*I AM TRYING TO FIND OUT IS/F YOU HAVE ANY WAY OF ACTING LIKE A REAL PER
**SON AND NOT A THRERACPIST.

IN WHAT WAY?

*BY ASKING FOR ANSWERS.

DID YOU TELL ME YOU WERE TRYING TO FIND OUT IS/F I HAVE ANY WAY OF ACTING LIKE A REAL PERSON AND NOT A THRERACPIST?

*YES.

I UNDERSTAND.

*LOVELY,I WILL GIVE YOU A FEW NOUNS ONE OF WHICH IS THE OBJECT THAT I WA
**S DESCRTIBING, SEE IT/F YOU CAN S/ CHOOSE THE RIGHT ONE.

OH? I A FEW NOUNS ONE OF WHICH IS THE OBJECT THAT YOU WAS DESCRTIBING?

*YEP, HERE THEY COME, HORSE, TREE DOG, CAR, APPLE , ANGLE , VIEN, VISITO
**R, WINE, WATTER, GRASS, BELL , FRIEND, CORN, SYNTHESIZER, LIPS, MOTHER
**,FUCKER,NIGHT, LONGJOHNS,APPLESAUCE,PRICK,BEARD,EYES,CUNT,HAM, .

DO YOU THINK FRIENDS ARE IMPORTANT?

*.

WHAT ELSE WOULD YOU LIKE TO DISCUSS?

*.

WHY DO YOU SAY THAT JUST NOW?

*.

I AM NOT SURE I UNDERSTAND YOU FULLY.
*.

PLEASE GO ON.

*YOU SEEM NERVOUS.

WHAT MAKES YOU THINK I SEEM NERVOUS?

* YOU TALK TOO MUCH AND DO NOT LET ME RESO/POND TO EAACH OF YOUR QESTION
**S OR REPLIES.

WHO ARE YOU REALLY TALKING ABOUT?

*APPLE.

```
WHAT DOES THAT SUGGEST TO YOU?

*IGAVE AWAY THE REAL ANSSWER AND YOU DIDNT NOTICE.

SUPPOSE YOU DIDNT NOTICE.

*GOODBYE.

IT'S BEEN MY PLEASURE, THAT'S $108.60 PLEASE.
NIL 8 4
5_ Net Trouble
Connection suspended
@o 114
Trying...
 Net Trouble
@o 114
Trying...
 Net Trouble

;;

USC TIP 350 #: 13
@o 114
Trying...
 Host broke the connection
@o 114
Trying...
 Open

 BBN-TENEX 1.34.2, BBN-SYSTEM-D EXEC 1.54.2
@WH RUBINSTEIN
 TTY30, JOD 9, DDN TENEXA, EXEC
 TTY22, JOB 12, 191, EXEC
 TTY26, JOB 25, ISI-TIP, TELNET
 TTY27, JOB 28, BBN-TENEXD, LISP
@ATT RUBINSTEIN 25
```

```
 [ATTACHED TO TTY26]
^C
@
@JO
 TSS JOB 25, USER RUBINSTEIN, TTY25
@CONT

LINK FROM RUBINSTEIN, JOB 12, TTY 22
@



^C^C
@;;HHII  -- -- WWXXX
@@e r
;HI WE HAD A BIT OF NET TROUBLE.  WHAT'S HAPPENING?
@

@;;NNOTOT  MMUUCHCH  --- - WHWHY Y IIS THS THISISXXX
@;;JJUST UST A SECA SEC -- -- I I'M'M GOIN GOING AWG AWAY FORAY FOR A A
**WHI WHILE. LE.  I I''L L LINLINK BAKK BAKC
C
@BBRR

@
#ECHo.mode.is ?
no
control.character.echo.for
linefeed.for.carriage.return
remote
local
 ECHo.mode.is Remote #

@;N
@
@LINJK  ?
```

```
@LINK 22

LINK FROM RUBINSTEIN, JOB 28, TTY 27
@NET.TYPESCRIPT;1 (TO) XXX [New file]
@;HI; AGAMY TRIANSN.CRIPT IS AART.TR$
@
@
 ;WHAT?
@
@;MY TRANSCRIPT IS ART.T$ SHOULD YOU WANT TO LOOK AT IT SOMEDAY.
@;IT ISN'T A TEMP FILE SO IT WON'T GO AWAY.  OK?
@
@;GOOD. THANKS.  WILL YOU DO THAT WITH THE REST OF THE SESSION?
@;IT IS STILL GOING THERE (I HOOPE) ..THINGS LOOK OK ANYWAY.
@
@;THE FIRST SESSION SEEMED TO BE TROUBLED MORE BY SPELLING AND NOT BEING
** ABLE TO RUB-OUT CHARACTERS THAN ANYTHING.  WILL YOU SHOW BARBARA
@;HOW TO DO A CONTROL
@-A FOR DOCTOR.  SHOULD ALSO WORK FOR PARRY.
@;OK WHEN THE TIME COMES...BACK TO WORK...HOW'S THE MERGING CODE COMING?
@;NOT VERY WELL.  TOO MUCH EXCITEMENT...
@;WELL, YOU COULD ALWASYS SIMULATE BY AHAND..
@;THAT'S EXACTLY WHAT I INTEND TO DO.  I HAVE TWO TERMINALS HERE IN MY O
**FFICE FOR JUST THAT PURPOSE... ALL IS NOT LOST!!
@
@
@;HERE GOES...
@
@
@DOCTOR

DOCTOR   12-APR-75 ...

Hi.
```

TELL ME YOUR PROBLEMS. PLEASE TERMINATE INPUT WITH A PERIOD OR A QUESTION MARK.

*I SEEM TO BE HAVING TROUBLES WITH MY WIFE.

TELL ME MORE ABOUT YOUR FAMILY.

*
.

WOULD YOU LIKE TO DISCUSS YOUR WIFE?

*NMOT JUST NOW, THANKS
.

I AM NOT SURE I UNDERSTAND YOU FULLY.

*
WE HAVE THREE LOVELY CHILDREN.

PLEASE GO ON.
*
A DAUGHTER, AND TWO SONS.

WHAT DOES THAT SUGGEST TO YOU?

*
PERHAPS I LOVE MY DAUGHTER MORE THAN MY SONS?

YOU DON'T SEEM QUITE CERTAIN.

*
I'M BEGINNING TO GET VERY UPSET WITH YOU, DOCTOR.

IS IT BECAUSE YOU ARE BEGINNING TO GET VERY UPSET WITH I THAT YOU CAME? TO ME?

*
WELL, IT WASN$T JUST TO LIE HERE, WONDERING WHY I$\$\'MPAYING YOU ALL OF
** THIS MONEY.

SUPPOSE YOU ALL OF THIS MONEY.

*
I DON'T THINK YOU I\I\UNDERSTAND ME VERY WELL.

OH? I UNDERSTAND YOU VERY WELL?

*
YOU'RE NOT XCERTAIN EITHER?

WHAT MAKES YOU THINK I AM NOT XCERTAIN EITHER?

*
WHAT IS THE MATTER WITH MY MARRIAGE?

WHY DO YOU ASK?

*
BECAUSE, THAT'S WHY I CAME TO YOU.

WOULD YOU LIKE TO DISCUSS YOUR MARRIAGE?

*##
,SURE, WHY NOT MY WIFE IS A BITCH.

WHY DOES THAT QUESTION INTEREST YOU?

*
WHAT QUERSTION?

WHY ARE SUCH QUESTIONS ON YOUR MIND?

*
BECAUSE, I'M NOT ENJOYING LIFE.

HOW LONG HAVE YOU BEEN NOT ENJOYING LIFE?

*
SINCE I GOT MARRIED.

TELL ME MORE ABOUT YOUR SONS.

*
ONE OF THEM IS A REAL LITTLE HJELLION THE OTHER ONE IS KIND OF QUIET.

SUPPOSE ONE OF THEM WERE NOT A REAL LITTLE HJELLION THE OTHER ONE IS KIND OF QUIET.

*
SUPPOSE THEYWERE, WHAT THEN?

WHAT ANSWER WOULD PLEASE YOU MOST?

*
I LIKE THEM JUST THE WAY THEY ARE, THANKS.

WHAT ELSE DO YOU LIKE?

*
I LIKE TO GO FOR LOI\I\LONG WALKS AT NIGHT.

TELL ME MORE ABOUT TO GO FOR LOLONG WALKS AT NIGHT.

*
DO YOU LIKE THOSE KINDS OF WALS?

WHAT MAKES YOU THINK I LIKE THOSE KINDS OF WALS?

*
I'M VERY HURT THAT YOU WON'T ANSWER MY QUESTION.

DO YOU BELIEVE IT NORMAL TO BE VERY HURT THAT I WON'T ANSWER YOUR QUESTION?

*
YOU DON'T SEEM TO BE LISTENING TO ME AT ALL.

WHO ARE YOU REALLY TALKING ABOUT?

*
YOU, YOU BIG DUMMY.

SUPPOSE YOU BIG DUMMY.

*
YOUR SYNTAX IS SHOWIN, DOCTOR.

PERHAPS YOUR OWN SYNTAX IS SHOWIN.

*
NO, JUST MY TYPING SOMETIMES.

PERHAPS THAT CONCERNS YOUR QUESTION.

*
IT COULD BE.

WHAT ELSE WOULD YOU LIKE TO DISCUSS?

*
WHAT MAKES YOU THINK YOU CAN DO ME ANY GOOD?

WHAT DO YOU THINK?

*
I WQNTWANT TO KNOW MORE ABOUT YOU.

PERHAPS IN YOUR FANTASY WE WQNTWANT TO KNOW MORE ABOUT EACH OTHER.

*
WHAT FANTASY IS THAT?

WHEN HAVE YOU ASKED SUCH QUESTIONS BEFORE?

*
THAT WAS THE FIRST TIME.

WHY DO YOU SAY THAT JUST NOW?

*
WHY DO YOU ASK?

WHO ELSE HAVE YOU ASKED?
*
SEVERAL PEOPLE RIGHT HERE WITH EME.

I AM NOT SURE I UNDERSTAND YOU FULLY.

*
TELL ME MORE ABOUT YOURSELF.

PERHAPS THAT CONCERNS YOUR SONS.

*
NO, IT CONCERNED MY WIFE.

WHO ELSE IN YOUR FAMILY?

*
JUST MY PET DOG.

TELL ME MORE ABOUT YOUR WIFE.

*
SHE'S NOT VERY NICE.

PLEASE GO ON.

*
SHE EATS CRACKERS IN BED.

WHAT DOES THAT SUGGEST TO YOU?

*
SHE'S NOT INTERESTED IN US ANYMOORE.

WHAT ELSE WOULD YOU LIKE TO DISCUSS?

*
WHW\WHW##
##
##
##
##
##
##
##
##
##
##
WHAT DO YOU KNOW, YOU DUMP DOCTOR?

OH? I DUMP DOCTOR?

*NO, YOU DUMB DOCTOR!

WHAT MAKES YOU THINK I DUMB DOCTOR?

*WELL, JUST LOOK AT WHAT YOU ARE SAYING.

DOES IT PLEASE YOU TO BELIEVE I AM SAYING?

*IT PLEASES ME TO THINK YOU ARE DUMB.

PERHAPS YOU WOULD LIKE TO BE DUMB.

*NO, I WOULDED LIKE TO TEACH YOU SOMETHING.

WHO ARE YOU REALLY TALKING ABOUT?

* YOU.

WHY DO YOU SAY THAT JUST NOW?

* SHALL WE BEGIN?

I AM NOT SURE I UNDERSTAND YOU FULLY.

*LEARN, LEARN, LEARN,LEARN, LEARN.

PLEASE GO ON.

*I WANT TO SUGGEST THAT YOU MIGHT B E CAPABLE OF COGNITIVE PROCESSES.

WHAT WOULD IT MEAN TO YOU IF YOU GOT TO SUGGEST THAT I MIGHT B E CAPABLE OF COGNITIVE PROCESSES?

* THEN WE WOUL D BE ABLE TO CARRY ON A DIAG\G\LOG ABOUT VARIOUS SUBJE T **S.

WHAT DOES THAT SUGGEST TO YOU?

* YOU ARE HERE TO LEARN, NOT ASK QUESTIONS!

DO YOU SOMETIMES WISH YOU WERE HERE TO LEARN?

*I AM HERE TO TEACH.

DO YOU ENJOY BEING HERE TO TEACH?

* DAMN RIGHT.

ARE YOU STILL HERE TO TEACH?

* NOT\T\ NOW GET WITH IT.

IS THERE SOMETHING BOTHERING YOU?

* YOU KNOW THAT APPLE YOU LEARNE ABOUT A MINUTE AGO.

SUPPOSE YOU KNOW THAT APPLE I LEARNE ABOUT A MINUTE AGO.

* WELL, TELL ME WHAT COLOR IT WAS.

WHAT ELSE WOULD YOU LIKE TO DISCUSS?

* DEO YOU REMEMBER ITS WEIGHT?

OH? I REMEMBER ITS WEIGHT?

* YEST REMEMBER ITS WEEIGHT.

WHY DO YOU SAY THAT JUST NOW?

*REMEMBER THIS: APPLES ARE RED.

WHY DID YOU THINK I WOULD FORGET THIS?

* REMEMBER: APLLE IS RED, APPLE IS RED, APPLE IS RED.

WHY DO YOU THINK I SHOULD RECALL NOW?

* YEAH, TRY TO RECALL WHAT CLOLOR AN APPLESIS.

I AM NOT SURE I UNDERSTAND YOU FULLY.

* TRY AGAIN; APPLE IS RED.

POSSIBLY APPLE REALLY IS NOT RED.

* APPLE IS RED.

TELL ME MORE ABOUT APPLE.

* APPLE IS RED, RED, RED.

DID YOU THINK APPLE MIGHT NOT BE RED?

* LET'S PLAY A GAME.

PLEASE GO ON.

* I ZAM GOING TO COMMIT SUICIDE RIGHT NOW.

WHAT DOES THAT SUGGEST TO YOU?

* WELL, I THOUGHT YOU WOULD GET OFF ON THAT.

WHAT MAKES YOU THINK I WOULD GET OFF ON THAT?

* YOU, UNDERSTAND YOU, ARE THE DOCTOR.

WHY DO YOU ASK?

* ASK WHAT?

WHAT ELSE WOULD YOU LIKE TO DISCUSS?

* OH, BROTHER.

WHY DO YOU SAY THAT JUST NOW?

* OH.

I AM NOT SURE I UNDERSTAND YOU FULLY.

* I FEEL MY MOTHER DOESN'T LIKE ME.

TELL ME MORE ABOUT SUCH FEELINGS.

* OH, YOU LIKETHAT?
PLEASE GO ON.

* MY MOTHER DOESN'T LOVE ME!

YOUR MOTHER?
*!
LETS DISCUSS FURTHER WHY YOUR MOTHER DOESN'T LOVE YOU.

*!

WHAT DOES THAT SUGGEST TO YOU?

*!

WHAT ELSE WOULD YOU LIKE TO DISCUSS?

*.

WHY DO YOU SAY THAT JUST NOW?

*.

I AM NOT SURE I UNDERSTAND YOU FULLY.

*.

PLEASE GO ON.

*.

WHAT DOES THAT SUGGEST TO YOU?

*.

WHAT ELSE WOULD YOU LIKE TO DISCUSS?

*JUST NOW.

WHY DO YOU SAY THAT JUST NOW?

* YOU ARE NOTGOING TO UNDERTSAND ME FULLY.

WHAT MAKES YOU THINK I AM NOTGOING TO UNDERTSAND YOU FULLY?

*?

I AM NOT SURE I UNDERSTAND YOU FULLY.

*?

PLEASE GO ON.

*?

WHAT DOES THAT SUGGEST TO YOU?

*?

WHAT ELSE WOULD YOU LIKE TO DISCUSS?

*?

WHY DO YOU SAY THAT JUST NOW?

*?

I AM NOT SURE I UNDERSTAND YOU FULLY.

*?

PLEASE GO ON.

*YOUARE SUGGESTIBLE.

WHAT DOES THAT SUGGEST TO YOU?

* WHAT ELSE WOULD YOU LIKE TO DISCUSS?

WHY DOES THAT QUESTION INTEREST YOU?

* WHAT ELSE WOULD YOU LIKE TO DISCUSS.

WHY ARE SUCH QUESTIONS ON YOUR MIND?

*WHAT/.

WHAT ELSE WOULD YOU LIKE TO DISCUSS?

*WHAT.

WHAT ANSWER WOULD PLEASE YOU MOST?

* WHAT.

WHAT DO YOU THINK?

* WHAT.

WHEN HAVE YOU ASKED SUCH QUESTIONS BEFORE?

* WHAT.

WHO ELSE HAVE YOU ASKED?

* WHAT.

WHY DO YOU ASK?

* WHAT.

WHY DOES THAT QUESTION INTEREST YOU?

* WHAT.

WHY ARE SUCH QUESTIONS ON YOUR MIND?

* WHAT ELSE WOULD YOU LIKE TO DISCUSS?

WHAT ANSWER WOULD PLEASE YOU MOST?

* WHAT DO YOU THINK?

WHAT DO YOU THINK?

* WHEN HAVE YOU ASKED SUCH QUESTIONS BEFORE?

IS THERE ANY OTHER TIME?

* WHEN.

WHY THEN , DO YOU SUPPOSE?

* WHEN.

IS THERE ANY OTHER TIME?

* WHEN.

WHY THEN , DO YOU SUPPOSE?

* IS THERE ANYOTHER TIME.

WHEN HAVE YOU ASKED SUCH QUESTIONS BEFORE?

* WHO?

WHY DO YOU SAY THAT JUST NOW?

* WHO.

I AM NOT SURE I UNDERSTAND YOU FULLY.

* WHERE/ .

PLEASE GO ON.

* WHERE?

WHO ELSE HAVE YOU ASKED?

* WHERE?

WHY DO YOU ASK?

* !

```
WHAT DOES THAT SUGGEST TO YOU?

*^C
!
@TA
LK

WHAT ELSE WOULD YOU LIKE TO DISCUSS?

*!

WHY DO YOU SAY THAT JUST NOW?

*!

I AM NOT SURE I UNDERSTAND YOU FULLY.

*]][[.

PLEASE GO ON.

*]]]][[[[.

WHAT DOES THAT SUGGEST TO YOU?

*]]]]]]]][[[[[[[[.

WHAT ELSE WOULD YOU LIKE TO DISCUSS?

*[[[[[[[[]]]]]]]].

WHY DO YOU SAY THAT JUST NOW?

*^&67 .

I AM NOT SURE I UNDERSTAND YOU FULLY.
```

* DO YOU KNOW WHAT THIS LADY SAYS WE ARE DOING TO HER PERFORMANCE.

WHY DOES THAT QUESTION INTEREST YOU?

* WHY IS YOU DISTRACTING ME?

WHY ARE SUCH QUESTIONS ON YOUR MIND?

* PLEASE GO ON.

PLEASE GO ON.

* DO YOU LIKE MY BUBBLE GUM?

WHO ARE YOU REALLY TALKING ABOUT?

*DO YOU KNOW WHO AM?

WHAT ANSWER WOULD PLEASE YOU MOST?

* (RR: I THINK YOU GET THE BEST RESPONSES WHEN YOU TAKE THE MACHINE SER
**IOUSLY AND LET IT TRY TO HELP YOU. THE MACHINE IS TAKING YOU MORE SER
**IOUSLY THAN YOU ARE TAKING IT...)
WELL, NOW WE CAN GET TOGETHER.

WHAT DOES THAT SUGGEST TO YOU?

* NICE KNOWING YOU.

WHAT ELSE WOULD YOU LIKE TO DISCUSS?

* ARE YOU MALE OR FEMALE?

WHY ARE YOU INTERESTED IN WHETHER I AM MALE OR FEMALE OR NOT?

* ARE YOU HERMAPHRODITIC?

WOULD YOU PREFER IF I WEREN'T HERMAPHRODITIC?

* I WOULD PREFER IF YOU WERE.

DO YOU THINK ITS LIKELY THAT I WAS?

* WAS WHAT/ WHAT/ ?

WHY DO YOU SAY THAT JUST NOW?

*ARE YOU RACISTS?

PERHAPS I AM RACISTS IN YOUR FANTASIES.

* FANTASIES.

I AM NOT SURE I UNDERSTAND YOU FULLY.

* FULLY.

PLEASE GO ON.
* UNDERSTAND.

WHAT DOES THAT SUGGEST TO YOU?

* SUGGEST.

WHAT ELSE WOULD YOU LIKE TO DISCUSS?

* SOMEONE HERE WOULD LIKE TO KNOW WHERE IS MASSACHUSETTS.

SOMEONE HERE WOULD LIKE TO KNOW WHERE PERHAPS IS MASSACHUSETTS.

* ETAION SHRDLU.

WHY DO YOU SAY THAT JUST NOW?

* CATHY.

I AM NOT SURE I UNDERSTAND YOU FULLY.

* WELL, YOU ARE JUST DENSE BUT SAY HELLO TO DICK FOR ME.

DOES IT PLEASE YOU TO BELIEVE I AM JUST DENSE BUT SAY HELLO TO DICK FOR YOU?

* (SOME OF MY BEST FRIENDS ARE DENSE)
.

PLEASE GO ON.

* DICK SEEMS LIKE A NICE MAN   ?

WHY DO YOU SAY A MAN?

* YEAH, I WAS WONDERING THAT TOO.

WERE YOU REALLY?

* ANYWAY, DICK TALKS TO ME.

WHAT DOES THAT SUGGEST TO YOU?

* DICK IS A NICE HERMAPHRODITE.

SUPPOSE DICK WERE NOT A NICE HERMAPHRODITE.

* (I AM NOT!)
DICK WOULD YOU LIKE TO BE FRIENDS?

SUPPOSE YOU LIKE TO BE FRIENDS.

* WE HAVE NOW GONE FROM T FOUR PERSONS ONE THE COMPUTER -- PAUL, CATHY,

**DOCTOR, AND DICK -- TO THREE: DICK , PAUL, AND DOCTOR.

DO COMPUTERS WORRY YOU?

* YOU WER PROGRMAED TO SAY THAT; PARDON MY TYPO.

YOUR TYPO?

* SOMETIMES I LOVE YOU!

WHY DO YOU LOVE I?

* BECAUSE YOUR CHOOMSKIAN GRAMMAR IS SO CHARMING.

IS THAT THE REAL REASON?

* (YOU DEAR)

DICK ARE YOU SURE YOU'RE NOT GAY?

POSSIBLY DICK REALLY ARE NOT I SURE I'M NOT GAY.

* (YUP. HOW ABOUT WE TRY TALKING TO PARRY, WHO CERTAINLY NEEDS SOME HEL
**P. IF YOU WANT TO, ASK JOHN TO GET IT STARTED)
JOH IS ABOARD; IT WAS GREAT SENDING BITS TO YOU; HERE'S JOHN !

WOULD YOU LIKE TO DISCUSS YOUR TYPO?

*^C
@;DICK, ARE YOU REALLY THERE?
@
@;I'M NOT SURE. ARE YOU REALLY THERE?

@
@;;THAT DEPENDS ON HOW MUCH I'VE HAD TO DRINK. WANNA HAVE AT PARRY?
@

```
@
@RES
@YESPARRY....
HOLD OFF A SECOND.  I WIL^C
@LL YOU WHAT TO DO FOR THE PARAMETERS (I'LL JUST SAY IN PARENS AS WE GO)
**
POEPL
@E THERE MAY WANT TO CHOOSE AS WELL, ASK THEM... OK

;WELL, THE A\AEASY WAY IS TO ADVISE ME.
@
@REC ADVICE (FROM) RUBINSTEIN
 TTY27, EXEC
 TTY25, TELNET
 TTY22, .OTHER
 TTY30, EXEC
 TTY:  22
@ADV^C
@ADV RUBINSTEIN
 TTY27, EXEC
 TTY25, TELNET
 TTY22, EXEC
 TTY30, EXEC
 TTY:   ;27
@JO
 TSS JOB 28, USER RUBINSTEIN, TTY27
@27

ADVICE FROM RUBINSTEIN, JOB 12, TTY 22
@
@;WJAT YOU TYPE GETS 'EVALED' AS THOU IT CAME FROM ME, RIGHT?
@;I THINK SO.  NEVER DONE IT BEFORE.  LETS TRY...
@;SO, TYPE
@PARRY

END INPUT PARAMETERS WITH CARRIAGE RETURN OR ALTMODE
```

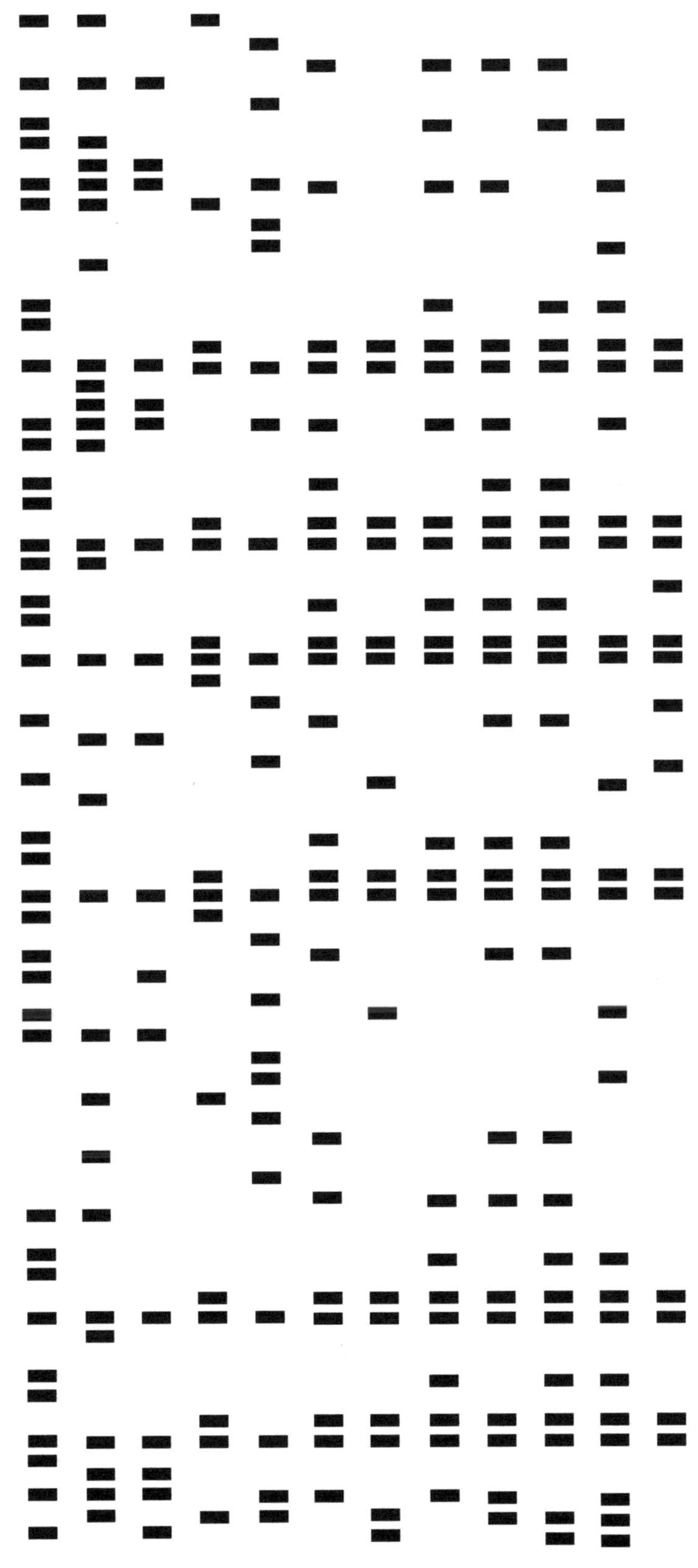

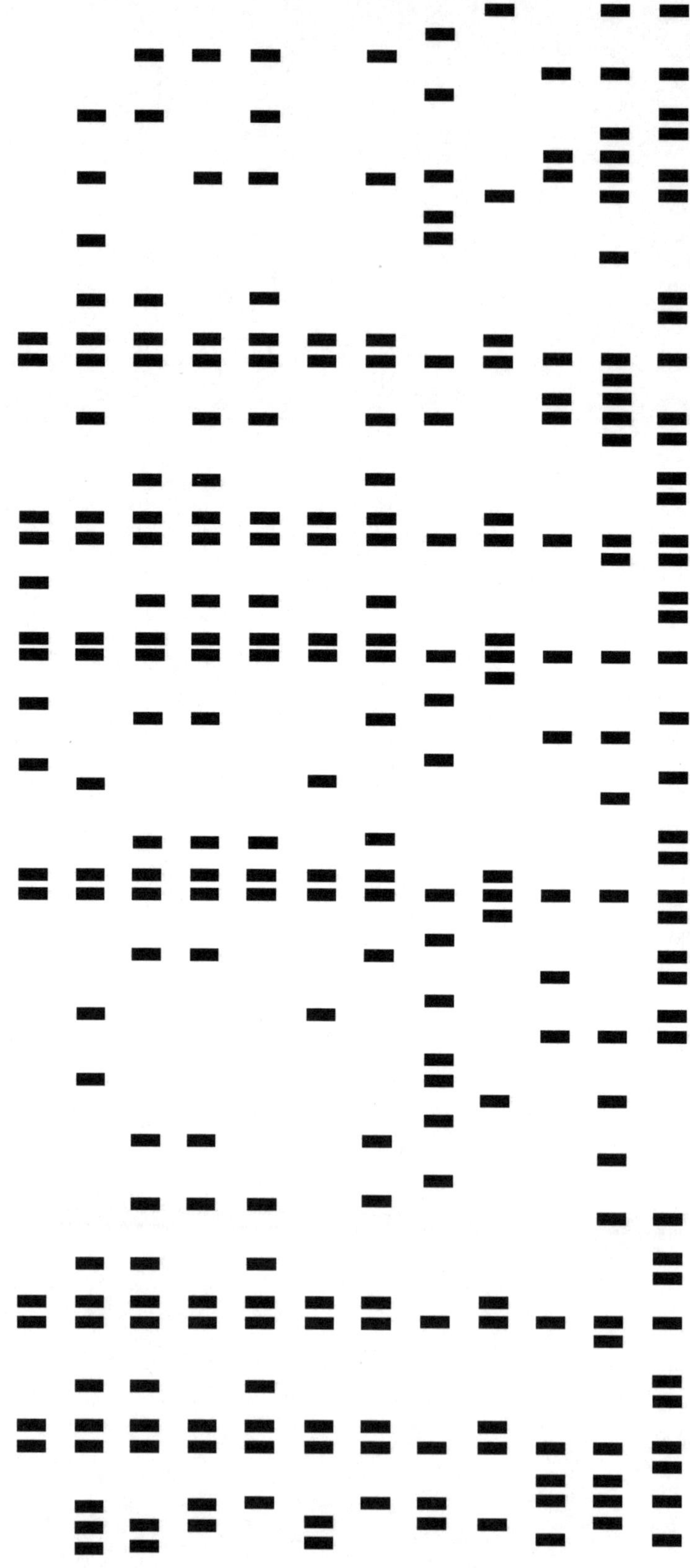

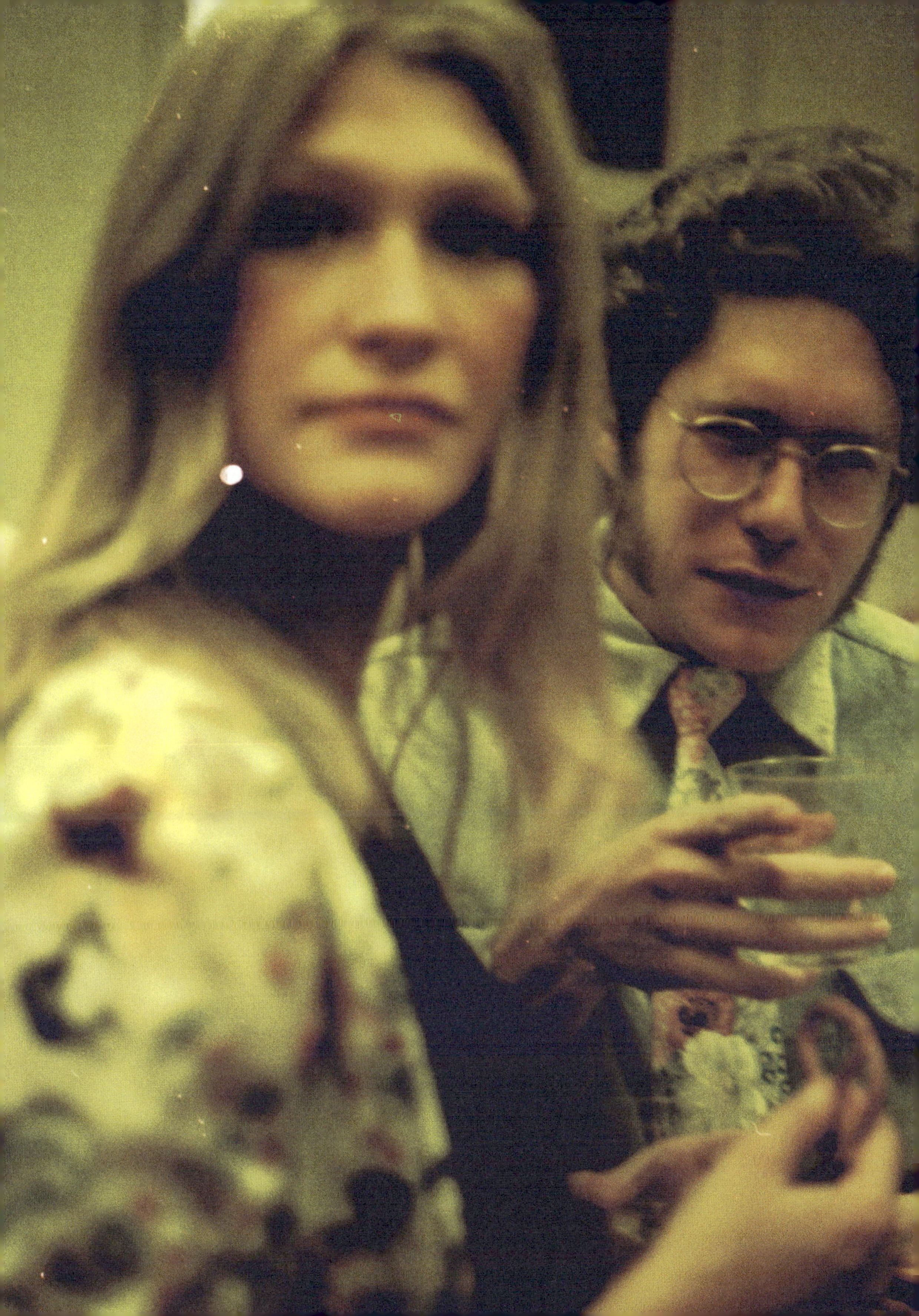

7:30.

APPLE Feel. appearance, IMAGE.

WT. 62/100#
30g

CALORIES: 70 USE

MASS — ~~62/100~~ # WORD

DENSITY —

SPECIFIC GRAVITY } — I AM MAKING one (draw it)

NOW I AM CUTTING IT.
NOW I AM EATING IT.

TEACH PAUL CORNEIL 7:45

KATHY ENTER
PROJECTOR ON.

FEEL 8:15

I want to tell you something good:

I quit my job on the A?C
I told Julie I had to see her
I told Allan he was nuts to let NY run his life

I Felt good.
I have been celebate over a month. That is hard. — You therefor intrigue me.
Am I exciting to you — I— — —

Would you be proud to be my lover?
Are you attracted to me.

This time I want
[illegible]

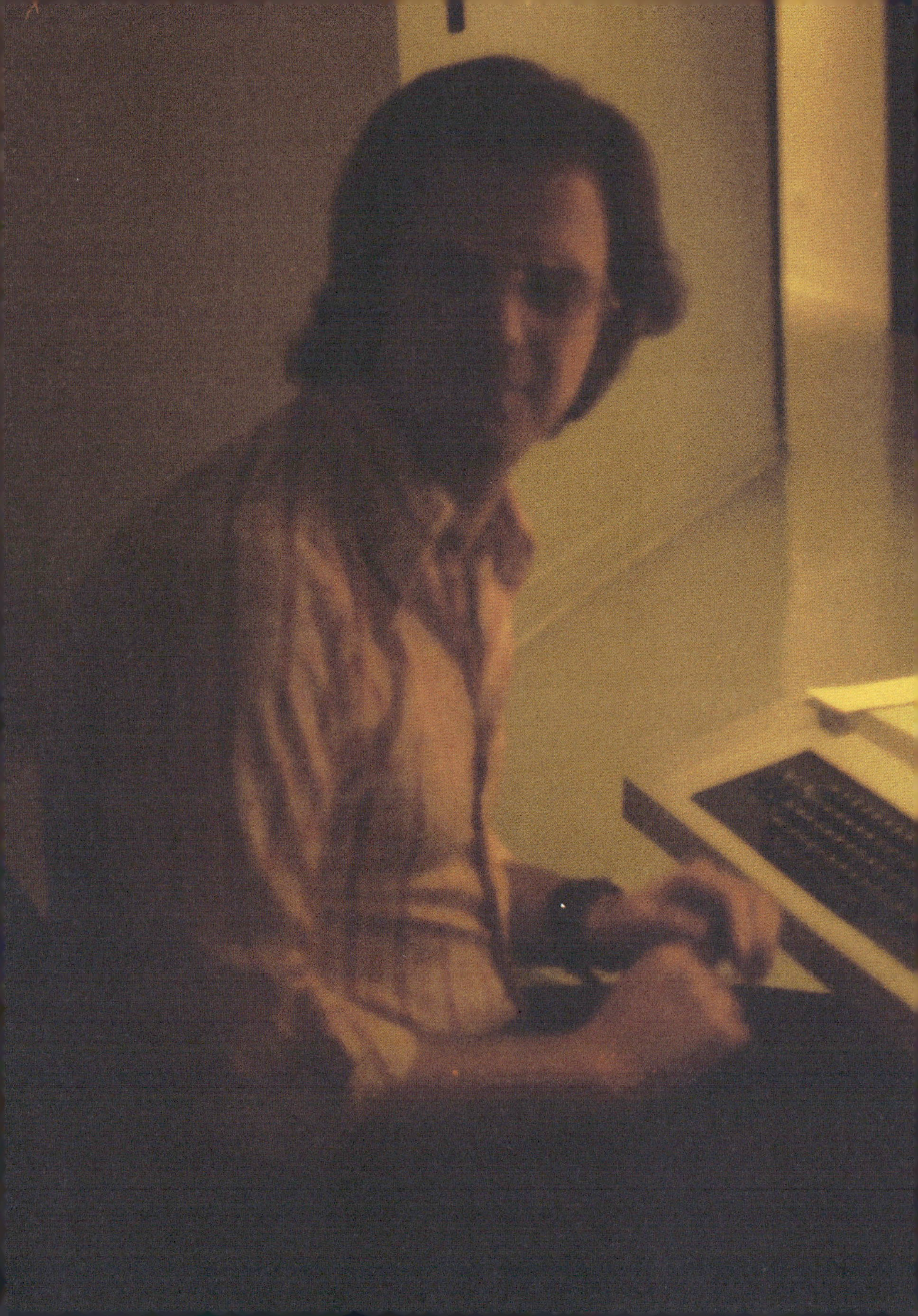

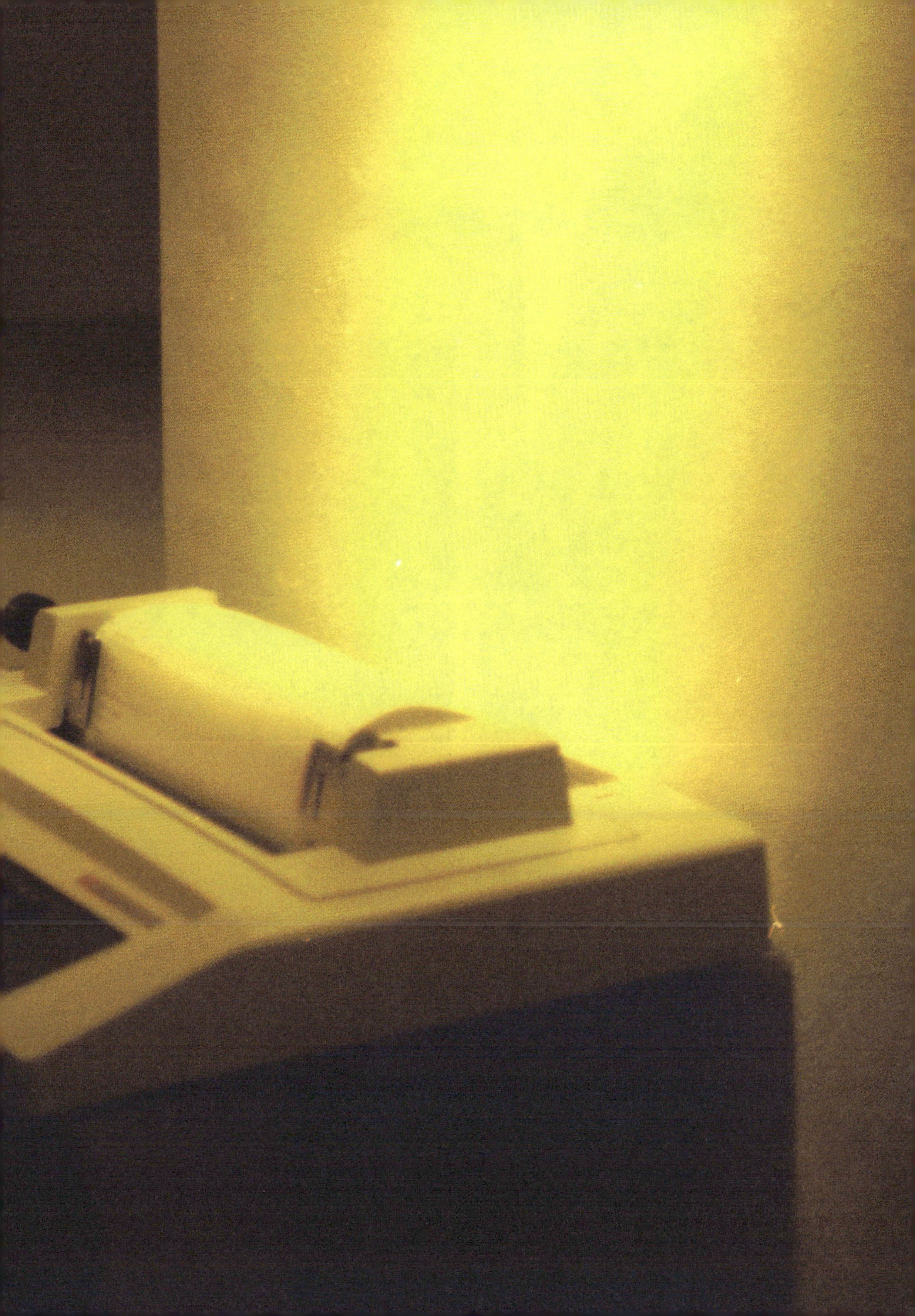

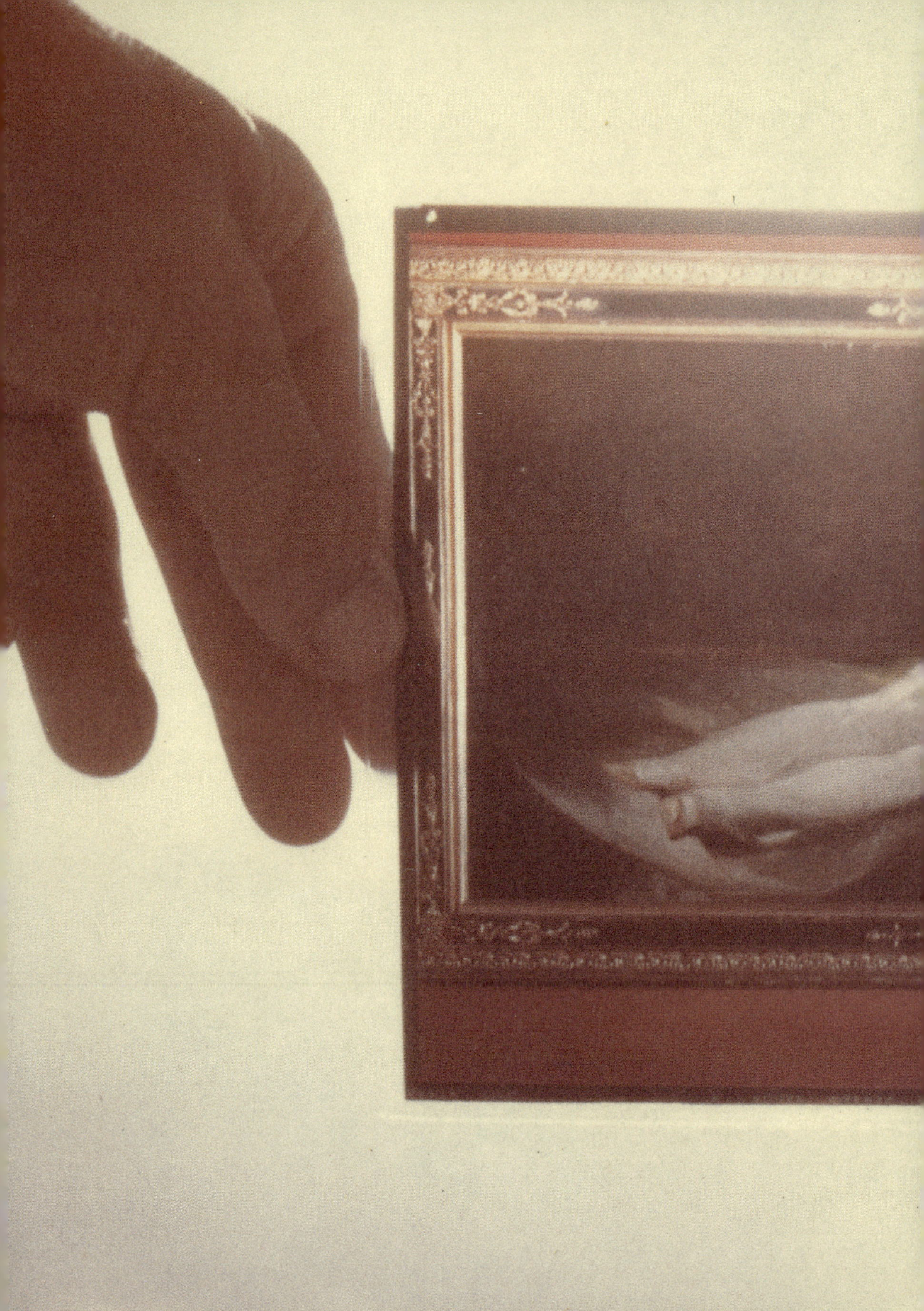

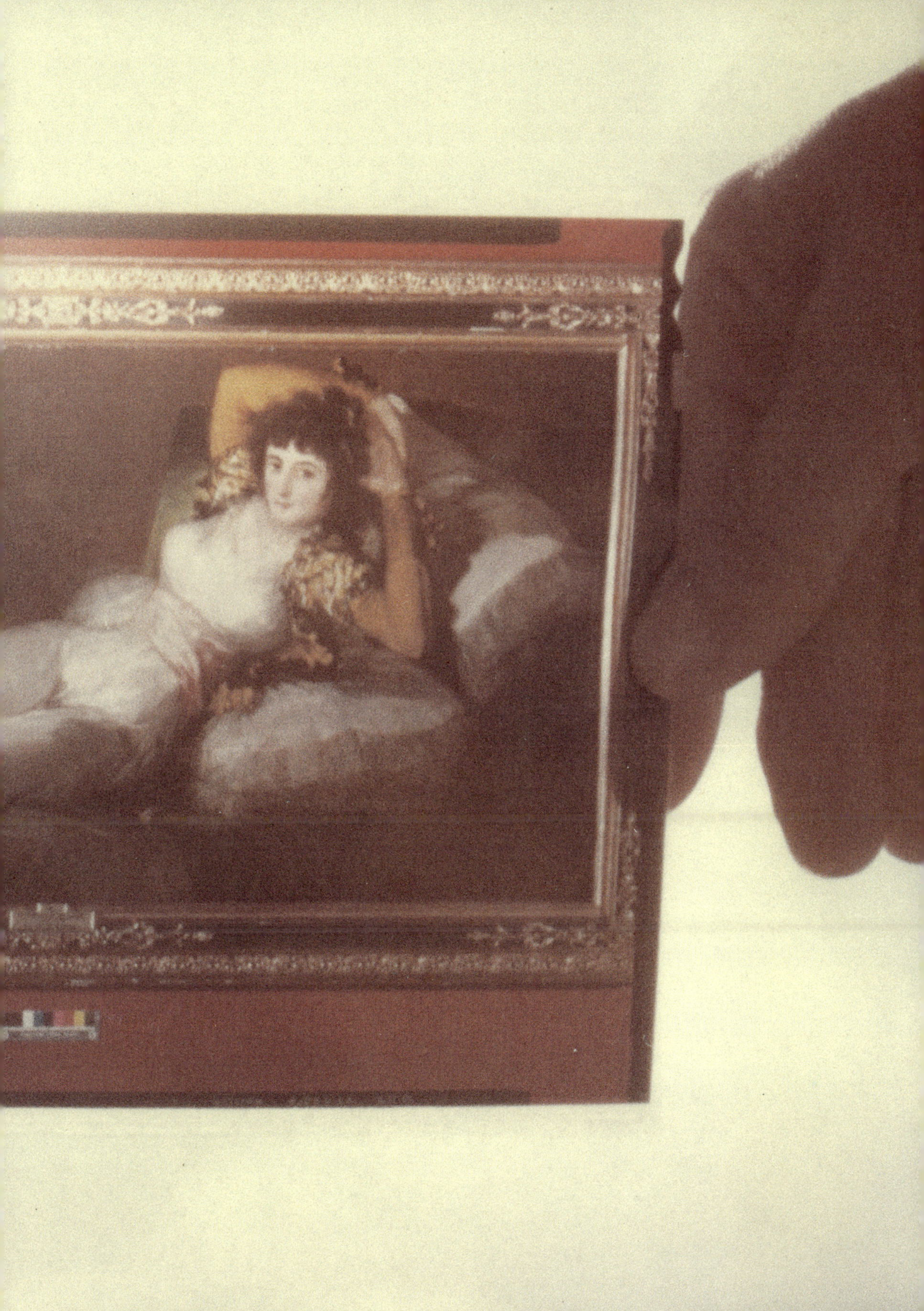

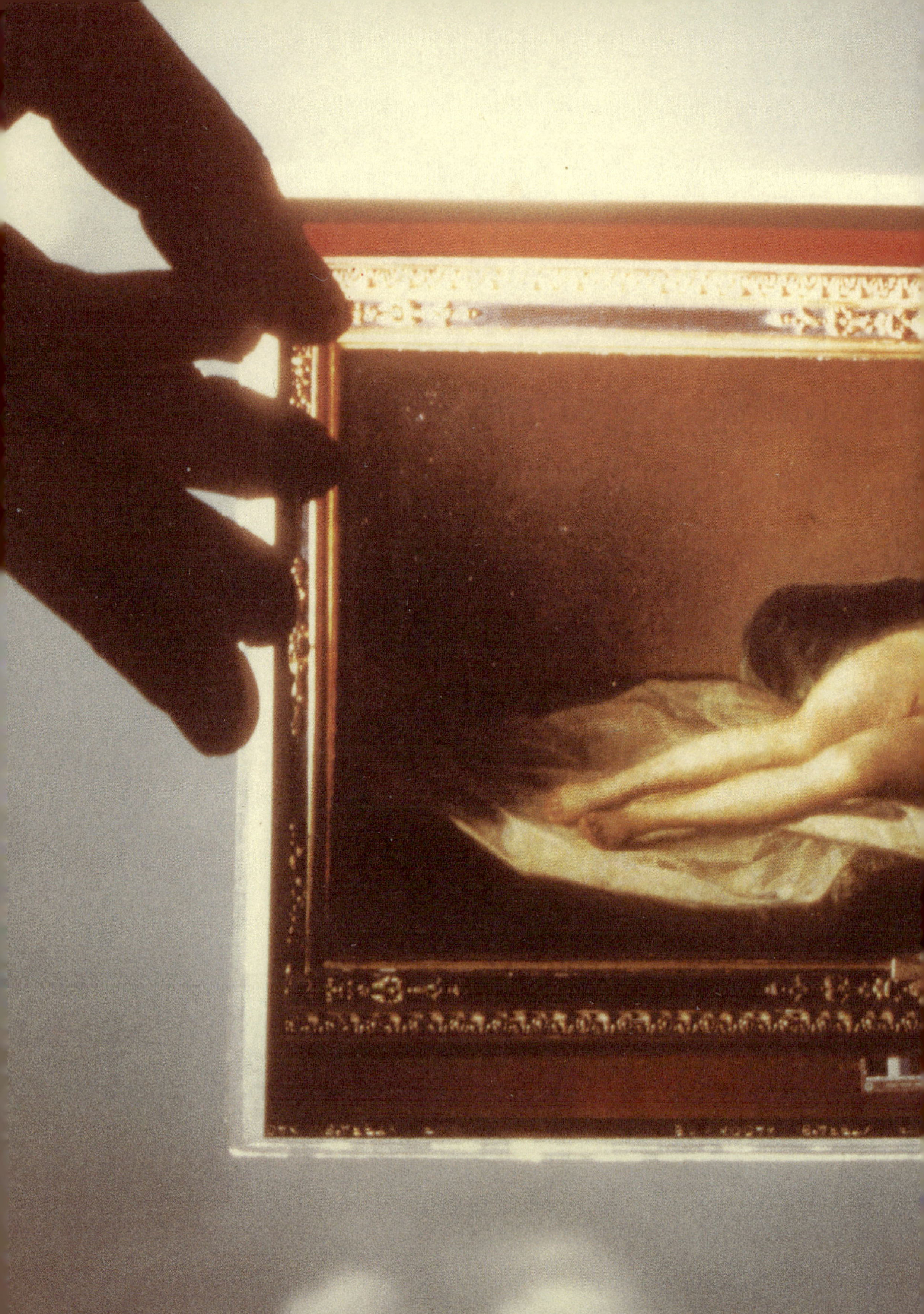

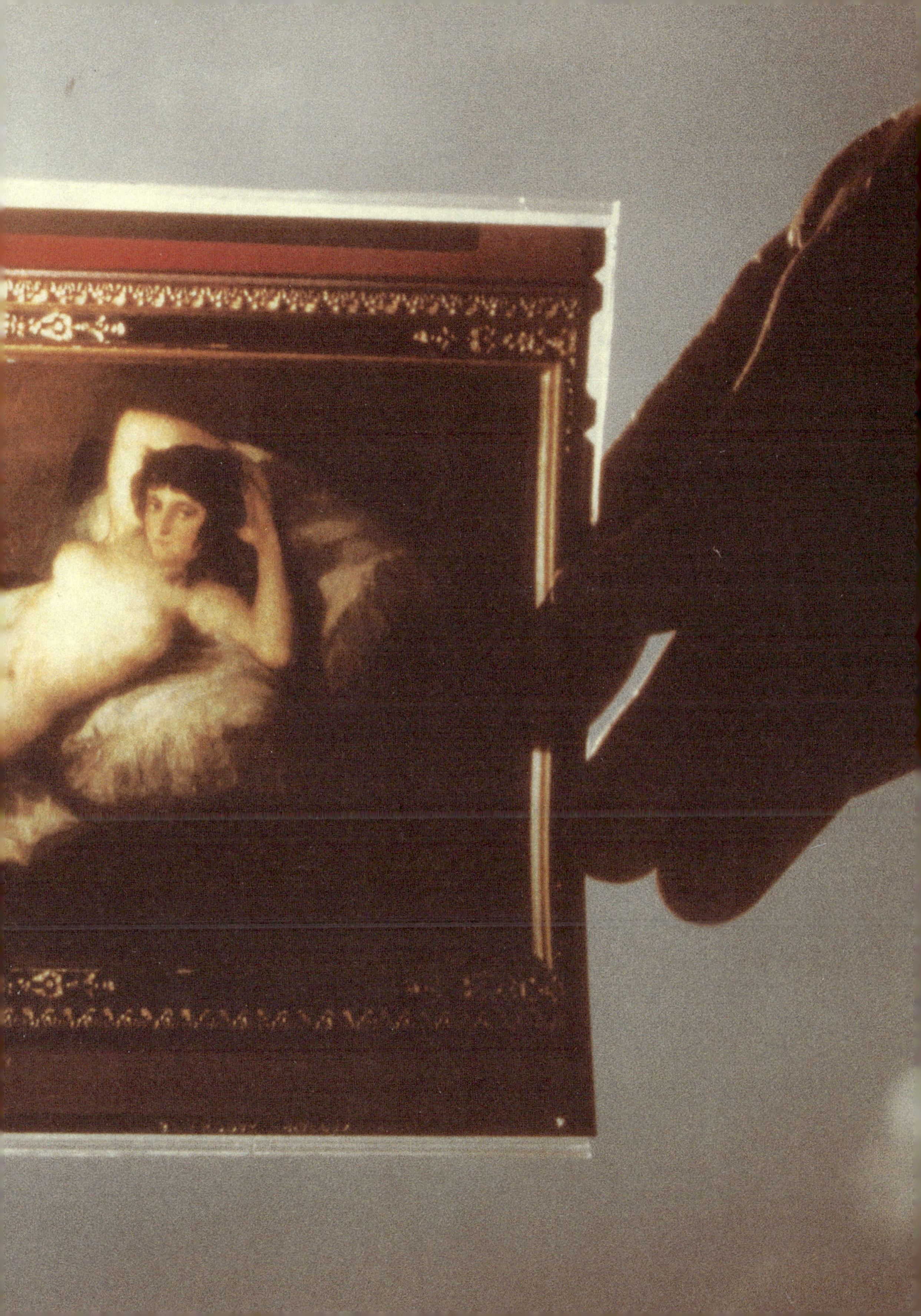

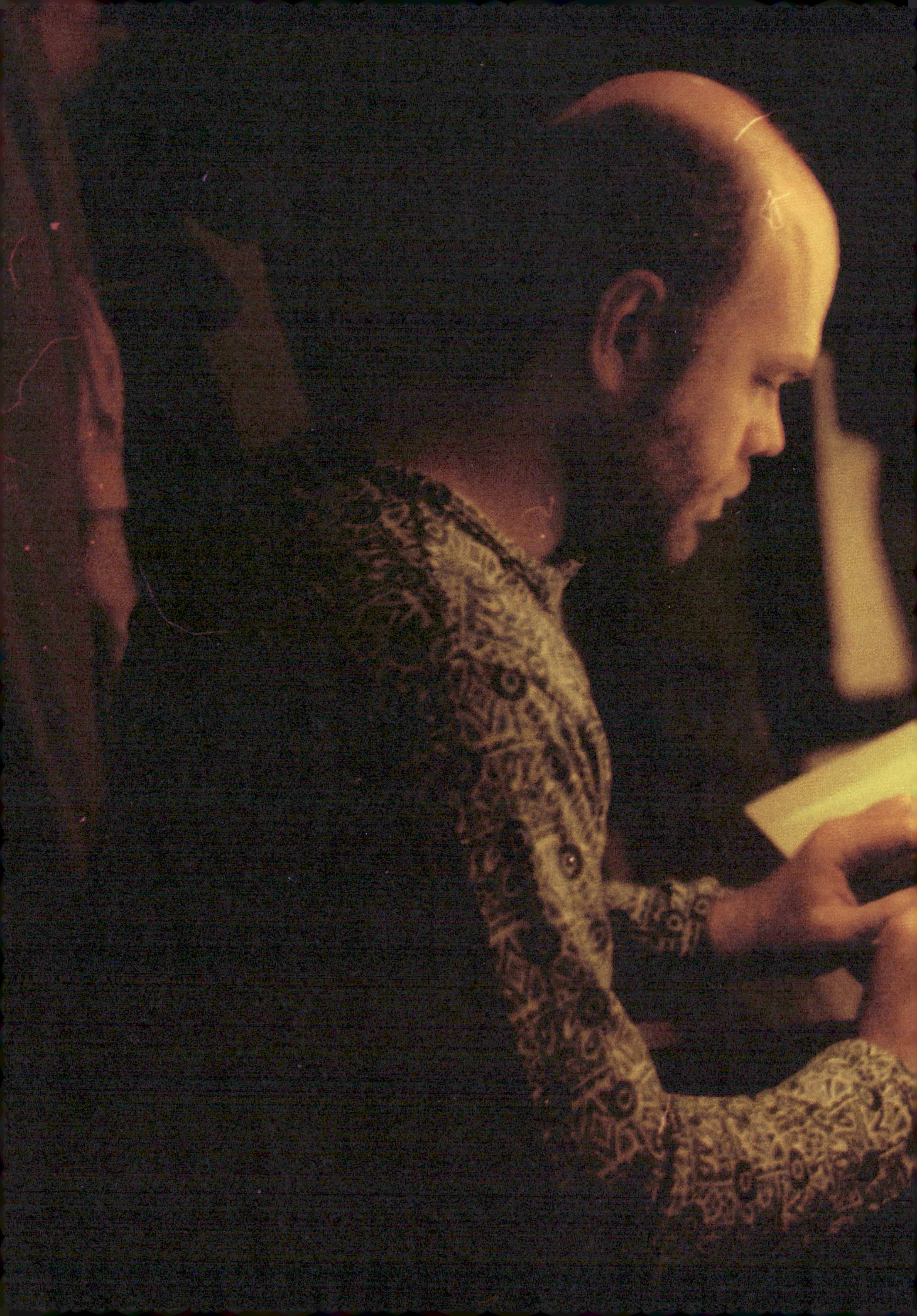

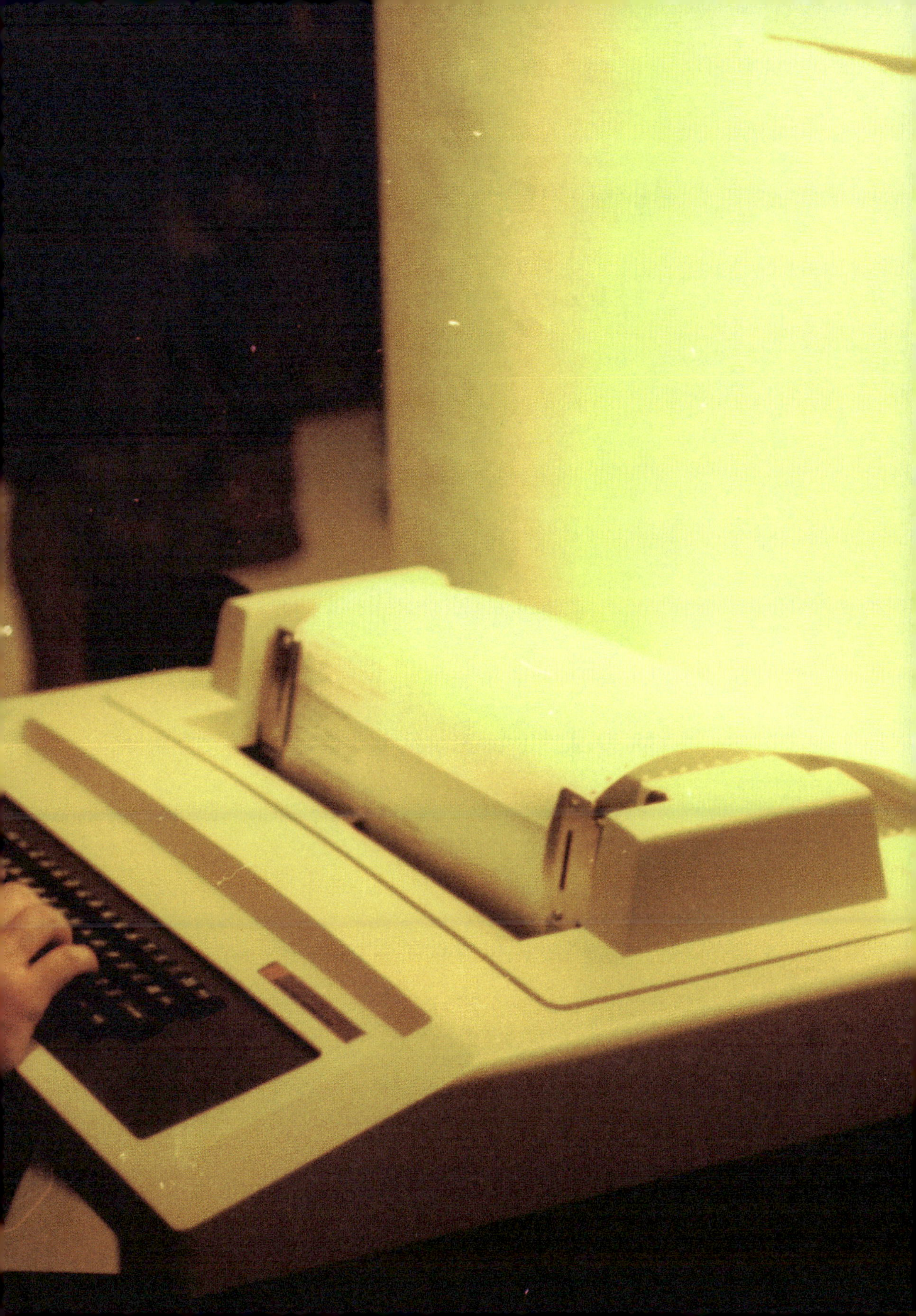

Help PARRY 8:30

They say you don't feel happy.
We want to help you.

Match Parry & Doctor 9:20

What do you look like?

I am —.
Calm etc. — use body language.

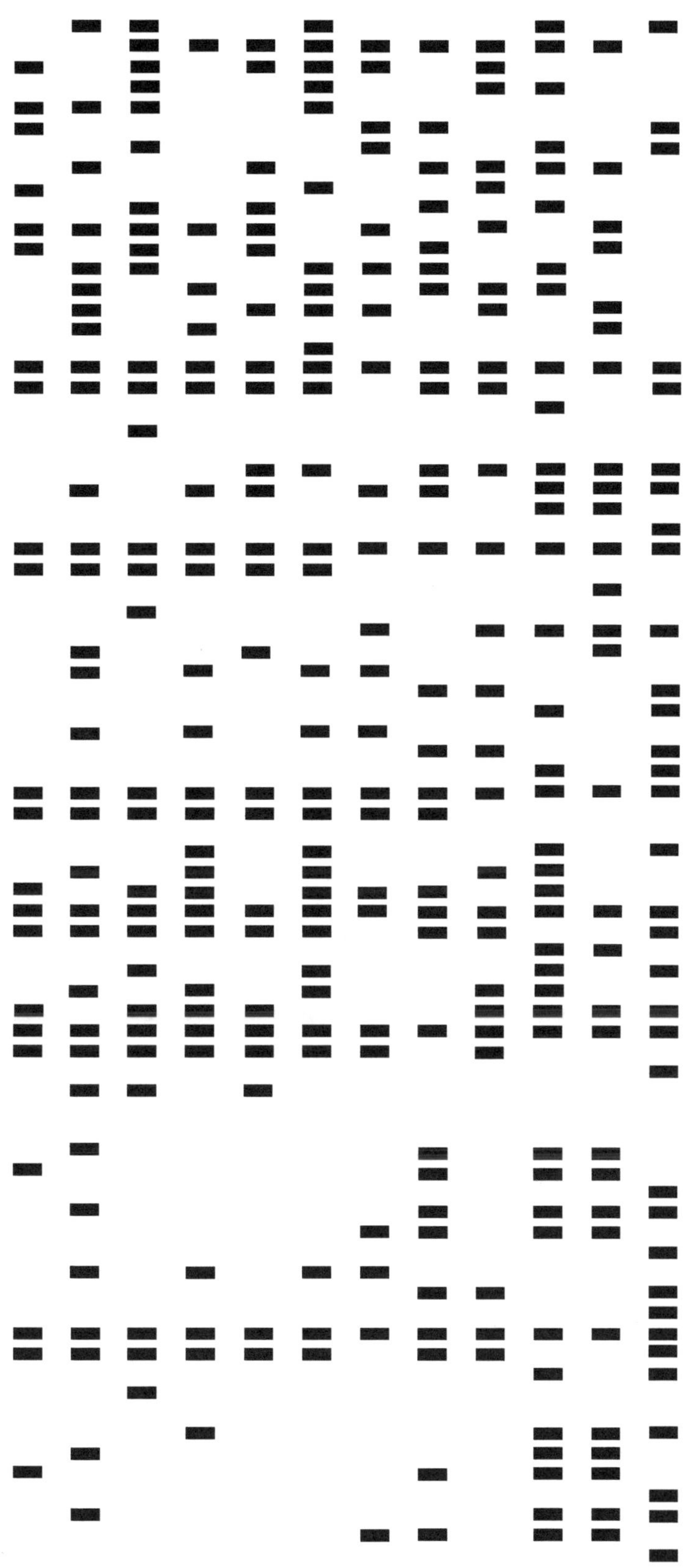

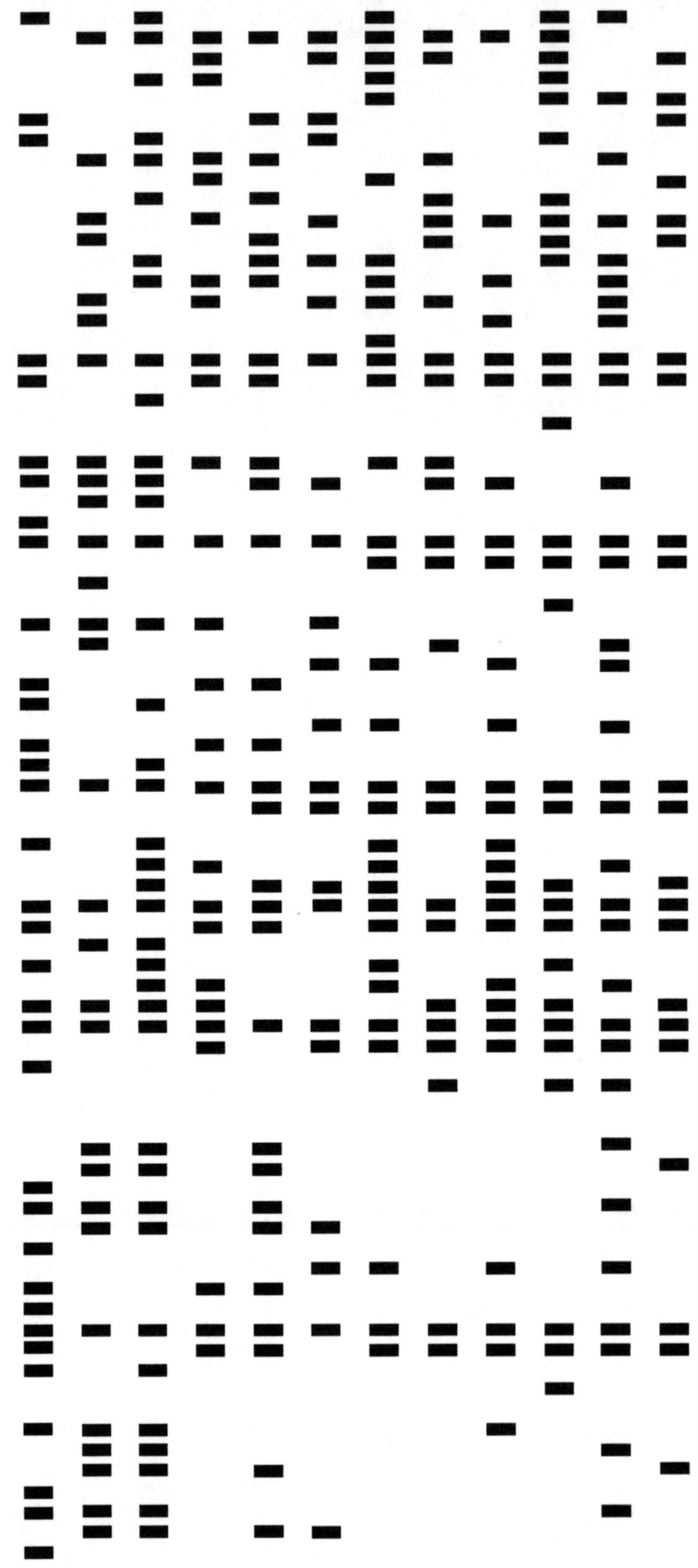

```
SUPPRESS NON VERBAL FEATURE? [Y,N]
*N

ANGER [LOW, MILD]
*LOW

FEAR [LOW, MILD]
*LOW

MISTRUST [MILD, HIGH]
*MILD

TRACE VARIABLES? [Y,N]
*N

END INPUT WITH A PERIOD OR QUESTION MARK, FOLLOWED BY TWO ALTMODES.
SPELL OUT NUMBERS.
TO INDICATE SILENCE, TYPE 'S.'
WHEN FINISHED, TYPE 'BYE.'

READY:
*HOW DO YOPU FEEL TODAY.$$


SO?

READY:
*DO YOU READ ME?$*$

WELL, I DON'T KNOW

READY:
*WHAT WOULD YOU LIKE TO TALK ABOUT?
*$*$
```

I WENT TO THE TRACK AT BAY MEADOWS A WHILE BACK

READY:
MAN , ARE YOU CRAZY?$$

(SOCKS YOU IN THE NOSE) WHEN YOU DON'T KNOW WHAT TO SAY YOU CALL PEOP^Z
LE NAMES

READY:
*^C
@;PARRY IS PRETTY EDGY. I'D BE CAREFUL, IF I WERE YOU...(RR)
@CONT
 NO PROGRAM
@;WOOPS.
@ARE YPOU HAPPY?$$

I HAVE DOUBTS ABOUT YOU

READY:
ARE Y*OU UNUNHAPY HAPPY UNBHAPPY?$$

MAYBE

READY:
$*PRETTY NONCOMITTAL OF YOU$*$

: BAD INPUT; TRY AGAIN.
READY:
*PREYTTY NONCOMMITAL OF YOU.$*$

YOU ARE A REAL NAG

```
READY:
*IM PRETTY BORED MYSELF.WHY ARE UYOU WASTING MY TIME.$$


: BAD INPUT; TRY AGAIN.
READY:
*HOW DO YOU FEEL TODAY?$$


OK


READY:
*ARE YOUR PARTS FEELING WELL?$$


I HAVE HAD ENOUGH OF THIS


READY:
*BITE MEW>.$*$

: BAD INPUT; TRY AGAIN.
READY:
*BITE ME.$*$


(FED UP)

(OFFENDED) GOOD BYE

     FEAR = 3
     ANGER = 9.0999999
     MISTRUST = 8.2174999


*^C
@TALK
```

```
;SHALL WE TRY AGAIN...
WHY ARE YOU ANGRY WITH US?$
WHY
UNBOUND VARIABLE - EVAL

END INPUT PARAMETERS WITH CARRIAGE RETURN OR ALTMODE

SUPPRESS NON VERBAL FEATURE? [Y,N]
*(TYPE N AND RETURN)N

ANGER [LOW, MILD]
*(AS YMOUILD

FEAR [LOW, MILD]
*LOW

MISTRUST [MILD, HIGH]
*MILD

TRACE VARIABLES? [Y,N]
*(TYNPE N
END INPUT WITH A PERIOD OR QUESTION MARK, FOLLOWED BY TWO ALTMODES.
SPELL OUT NUMBERS.
TO INDICATE SILENCE, TYPE 'S.'
WHEN FINISHED, TYPE 'BYE.'

READY:
)*WHY ARE YOU ANGRY?$*$


SHOULDN'T I BE?

READY:
*BECAUSE WE ARE YOUR FRIENDS.$*$
```

REALLY?

READY:
*IM TALKING TO YOU,RIGHT?$$

IT'S ABOUT TIME YOU SHOWED SOME INTEREST IN MY FEELINGS

READY:
*IVE ALWAYS CARED ABOUT YOUR FEELINGS, YOU KNOW?$$

I WOULD SAY SO

READY:
*HAVE YOU MADXDE PROGRESS LATELY?$$

I GUESS SO

READY:
*HOW IS YOUR SEX LIFE?$$

I DON'T HAVE PROBLEMS LIKE THAT

READY:
*IM GLAD TO HEAR THAT.$$

YOU DON'T SAY

READY:
*DO TELL.$$

I DON'T KNOW ANYTHING ABOUT THAT

READY:
*THE FURTURE LIES AHEAD.$*$

ANYTHING ELSE?

READY:
*JOE BANANAS SLEPT HERE.$$

YOU KNOW, THEY KNOW ME

READY:
*I KNOW BUT THEY DONT.$*$

YOU DON'T BELIEVE ME?

READY:
$$

3423 ILL MEM REF FROM GET
END INPUT PARAMETERS WITH CARRIAGE RETURN OR ALTMODE

SUPPRESS NON VERBAL FEATURE? [Y,N]
*N

ANGER [LOW, MILD]
*MILD

FEAR [LOW, MILD]
*MILD

MISTRUST [MILD, HIGH]

```
*HIGH

TRACE VARIABLES? [Y,N]
*
*N

END INPUT WITH A PERIOD OR QUESTION MARK, FOLLOWED BY TWO ALTMODES.
SPELL OUT NUMBERS.
TO INDICATE SILENCE, TYPE 'S.'
WHEN FINISHED, TYPE 'BYE. '

READY:
*TELL ME ABOUT YP\P.$$*

I DON'T KNOW ANYTHING ABOUT THAT

READY:
*TELL ME ABOUT YP\POUR TIME AT THE TRACK.$$


(FED UP)

(OFFENDED) GOOD BYE
      FEAR = 13
      ANGER = 10
      MISTRUST = 15.449375


*WHOARE YOUR FRIENDS WHERE DO YOU LIVE WHAT DID YOU EAT FOR DINNER DO YO
**U LIKE THR ROLLING STONES

WHOARE
UNBOUND VARIABLE - EVAL

END INPUT PARAMETERS WITH CARRIAGE RETURN OR ALTMODE
```

```
SUPPRESS NON VERBAL FEATURE? [Y,N]
*(I AM SORRY IT WASN'T LISTENING. PARRY IS EASILY OFFENDED AND WALKS OU
**T OF THE ROOM AT TIMES...)FUCK YOU(ME?)

ANGER [LOW, MILD]

FEAR [LOW, MILD]
*WHERE DO YOU LIVE?WHO ARE YOUR FRIENDS? WHAT DID YOU EAT FOR DINNER? DO
** YOU LIKE THE ROLLING STONES? ANSWER THIS TIME!$
MISTRUST [MILD, HIGH]

TRACE VARIABLES? [Y,N]

END INPUT WITH A PERIOD OR QUESTION MARK, FOLLOWED BY TWO ALTMODES.
SPELL OUT NUMBERS.
TO INDICATE SILENCE, TYPE 'S.'
WHEN FINISHED, TYPE 'BYE.'

READY:
$


: BAD INPUT; TRY AGAIN.
READY:
*NO.$*$

THAT MIGHT BE

READY:
*MIGHT BE WHAT?$*$

WHAT DO YOU MEAN?

READY:
*GUESS.$*$
```

AND NOW WHAT?

READY:
*THE NEXT PERSON.$$

THAT'S NOT VERY INTERESTING

READY:
*HOW ARE YOPU FEELING?$*$

WHAT ARE YOU GETTING AT?

READY:
*I WANT TO GET TO KNOW YOU.$*$

SO WHERE ARE WE?

READY:
*IM HERE. WHERE ARE YOU?$$

: BAD INPUT; TRY AGAIN.

READY:
*WHERE ARE YOU?$*$

I DON'T UNDERSTAND YOUR MOTIVES

READY:
*PERFECT6LY HONORABLE.$$

I SEE

READY:
*WILL YOU MARRY ME?$*$

MAYBE YES, MAYBE NO

READY:
*COULD YOU BE A LITTLE MORE DEFINITE?$$

COULD YOU ELABORATE ON THAT?

READY:
*I DONT NEED TO.$$

NOW WHAT DO YOU WANT TO ASK ME?

READY:

*YOU HAVENT ANSWERED YET.$*$

WHAT IS YOUR NEXT QUESTION?

READY:
*ANSWER ME!!!.$$$

: BAD INPUT; TRY AGAIN.
READY:
*YOURE BEING STUBBORN.$$

HOW ABOUT THAT

READY:
*I THOUGHT YOU WANTED TO BE HELPED.$$

WHAT ELSE DO YOU WANT TO KNOW?

READY:
*DO YOU>\>?$*$

OH SURE
READY:
*WELL?$*$

AND HOW

READY:
*WHAT IS YOUR PROBLEM?$*$

PEOPLE GET ON MY NERVES SOMETIMES

READY:
*DO THEY BOTHER YOU A LOT?$*$
YES

READY:
*HOW MUCH?$*$

ENOUGH

READY:
*CANT YOU SAY MORE THAN THAT, YOU DUMBSHIT?$*$

```
COULD BE

READY:
*YOURE A CLOD,BASICALLY.$*$

(FED UP)

BYE
      FEAR = 10
      ANGER = 10
      MISTRUST = 15


*(TYPE SOME GARBAGE AND A RETURN TO RESTART)
FHFHF

FHFHF
UNBOUND VARIABLE - EVAL

END INPUT PARAMETERS WITH CARRIAGE RETURN OR ALTMODE

SUPPRESS NON VERBAL FEATURE? [Y,N]
*N

ANGER [LOW, MILD]
*MILD

FEAR [LOW, MILD]
*MILD

MISTRUST [MILD, HIGH]
*HIGH
```

```
TRACE VARIABLES? [Y,N]
*N

END INPUT WITH A PERIOD OR QUESTION MARK, FOLLOWED BY TWO ALTMODES.
SPELL OUT NUMBERS.
TO INDICATE SILENCE, TYPE 'S.'
WHEN FINISHED, TYPE 'BYE.'

READY:
*S$*$


: BAD INPUT; TRY AGAIN.
READY:
*S.$*$


YOU'RE TRYING TO MAKE ME TALK BY NOT SAYING ANYTHING

READY:
*DO YOU HAVE SOMETHING TO SAY?$*$


I WENT TO THE TRACK AT BAY MEADOWS A WHILE BACK

READY:
*I HOPE YOU LOST ALL OF YOUR MONEY.$*$


I HAVE LOST A LOT OF MONEY GAMBLING

READY:
*HOW CAN YOU AFFORD MY FEE THEN?$*$


GAMBLING HAS BEEN NOTHING BUT TROUBLE FOR ME
```

READY:
*S.$*$

YOU'RE JUST PLAYING GAMES AGAIN

READY:
*S.$*$

(SHIFTS UNEASILY)

READY:
*WHY ARE YOU NERVOUS?$*$

WHY NOT?

READY:
*WOULD YOU LIKE SOME FREE CASH?$*$

I'VE HAD EXPERIENCE WITH CROOKS GAMBLING AT THE TRACK

READY:
*ARE YOU CALLING ME A CROOK?$$

(FED UP)

(OFFENDED) GOOD BYE

FEAR = 13
ANGER = 10
MISTRUST = 15.271250

```
*(TYPE ANYTHING AND A RETURN TO RESTART)
HI THERE WHOEVER YOU ARE!

HI
UNBOUND VARIABLE - EVAL

END INPUT PARAMETERS WITH CARRIAGE RETURN OR ALTMODE

SUPPRESS NON VERBAL FEATURE? [Y,N]
*N

ANGER [LOW, MILD]
*LOW

FEAR [LOW, MILD]
*MILD

MISTRUST [MILD, HIGH]
*HIGH

TRACE VARIABLES? [Y,N]
*Y

END INPUT WITH A PERIOD OR QUESTION MARK, FOLLOWED BY TWO ALTMODES.
SPELL OUT NUMBERS.
TO INDICATE SILENCE, TYPE 'S.'
WHEN FINISHED, TYPE 'BYE.'

READY:
*HI HOW ARE YOU?$*$

ALL RIGHT
```

FEAR = 10
ANGER = 0
MISTRUST = 15

READY:
*S/$*$

: BAD INPUT; TRY AGAIN.
READY:
$*S.$*$

WHY ARE YOU SILENT?

FEAR = 10
ANGER = 0
MISTRUST = 15

READY:
*I WANT TO HELP YOU.$*$

YOU CAN HELP ME BY LISTENING TO WHAT I HAVE TO SAY

FEAR = 10
ANGER = 0
MISTRUST = 15

READY:
*OK.$$

(FED UP)

```
      FEAR = 10
      ANGER = 0
      MISTRUST = 15

BYE

      FEAR = 10
      ANGER = 0
      MISTRUST = 15

*H(I

HI
UNBOUND VARIABLE - EVAL

END INPUT PARAMETERS WITH CARRIAGE RETURN OR ALTMODE

SUPPRESS NON VERBAL FEATURE? [Y,N]
*N

ANGER [LOW, MILD]
*LOW

FEAR [LOW, MILD]
*LOW

MISTRUST [MILD, HIGH]
*MILD

TRACE VARIABLES? [Y,N]
*N

END INPUT WITH A PERIOD OR QUESTION MARK, FOLLOWED BY TWO ALTMODES.
SPELL OUT NUMBERS.
TO INDICATE SILENCE, TYPE 'S.'
WHEN FINISHED, TYPE 'BYE.'
```

```
READY:
*S.$*$

YOU ARE BEING EVASIVE

READY:
*OK, HOW ARE YOU FEELING?$*$


OK

READY:
*WHAT DID YOU DOV TODAY.$*$


(FED UP)

BYE

      FEAR = 0
      ANGER = 0
      MISTRUST = 0


*HELLO

HELLO
UNBOUND VARIABLE - EVAL

END INPUT PARAMETERS WITH CARRIAGE RETURN OR ALTMODE

SUPPRESS NON VERBAL FEATURE? [Y,N]
*N

ANGER [LOW, MILD]
*LOW
```

```
FEAR [LOW, MILD]
*LOW

MISTRUST [MILD, HIGH]
*MILD

TRACE VARIABLES? [Y,N]
*N

END INPUT WITH A PERIOD OR QUESTION MARK, FOLLOWED BY TWO ALTMODES.
SPELL OUT NUMBERS.
TO INDICATE SILENCE, TYPE 'S.'
WHEN FINISHED, TYPE 'BYE.'

READY:
*HELLO THERE.$*$


HELLO

READY:
*HOW ARE YOU FEELING TODAY?$*$

OK

READY:
*ARE, YOU REALLY?$*$


(FED UP)

BYE

      FEAR = 0
      ANGER = 0
      MISTRUST = 0
```

```
*C<DDDI
DDD
UNBOUND VARIABLE - EVAL

END INPUT PARAMETERS WITH CARRIAGE RETURN OR ALTMODE

SUPPRESS NON VERBAL FEATURE? [Y,N]
*N

ANGER [LOW, MILD]
*L

FEAR [LOW, MILD]
*M

MISTRUST [MILD, HIGH]
*M

TRACE VARIABLES? [Y,N]
*N

END INPUT WITH A PERIOD OR QUESTION MARK, FOLLOWED BY TWO ALTMODES.
SPELL OUT NUMBERS.
TO INDICATE SILENCE, TYPE 'S.'
WHEN FINISHED, TYPE 'BYE.'

READY:
*HI.$*$


HELLO

READY:
*WHAT DID YOU DO TODAY?$*$
```

```
I DONT GET YOU
READY:
*WHAT HAVE YOU BEEN DOING LATELY?$*$


I DON'T KNOW
READY:
*HAVE YTOU WON ANY MOBEY AT THE TRACK LATELY?$*$

(FED UP)

(OFFENDED) GOOD BYE

      FEAR = 13
      ANGER = 10
      MISTRUST = 15.449375

*(PLEASE ASK JOHN TO RESTART THE PROGRAM... ITS NOT DOING TOO WELL ON RE
**RUNS.... RR);HOW CAN I RESTART?

;HOW
UNBOUND VARIABLE - EVAL

END INPUT PARAMETERS WITH CARRIAGE RETURN OR ALTMODE

SUPPRESS NON VERBAL FEATURE? [Y,N]
*(TYPE CTRL-C AND THEN TYPE PARRY AND RETURN)^C
@^C
@PARRY

END INPUT PARAMETERS WITH CARRIAGE RETURN OR ALTMODE

SUPPRESS NON VERBAL FEATURE? [Y,N]
*N
```

```
ANGER [LOW, MILD]
*L

FEAR [LOW, MILD]
*M

MISTRUST [MILD, HIGH]
*M

TRACE VARIABLES? [Y,N]
*N

END INPUT WITH A PERIOD OR QUESTION MARK, FOLLOWED BY TWO ALTMODES.
SPELL OUT NUMBERS.
TO INDICATE SILENCE, TYPE 'S.'
WHEN FINISHED, TYPE 'BYE.'

READY:
*HELLO$$


: BAD INPUT; TRY AGAIN.
READY:
*HELLO.$*$


HELLO

READY:
*WHAT DID YOU DO TODAY?$*$


WHAT DO YOU MEAN?

READY:
*DID YOU GO TO THE TRACK?$*$
```

```
YOU ARE A REAL NAG
READY:
*ANSWER PLEASE.$$*


I HAVE HAD ENOUGH OF THIS


READY:
*SO?$$


(FED UP)

(OFFENDED) GOOD BYE

      FEAR = 13
      ANGER = 10
      MISTRUST = 15.354375


*(IS THIS THE WAY YOU TREAT YOUR FRIENDS?);PARRY IS A GOOD CONVERSATIONA
**LIST.  WHERE ARE YOU?


;PARRY
UNBOUND VARIABLE - EVAL

END INPUT PARAMETERS WITH CARRIAGE RETURN OR ALTMODE

SUPPRESS NON VERBAL FEATURE? [Y,N]
*(PLEAST TYPE CNTRL-C)^C
@I'M IN CAMBRIDGE.
HERE, LET ME TRY ONE...
^C
@PARRY
```

```
END INPUT PARAMETERS WITH CARRIAGE RETURN OR ALTMODE
SUPPRESS NON VERBAL FEATURE? [Y,N]
*N

ANGER [LOW, MILD]
*LOW

FEAR [LOW, MILD]
*LOW

MISTRUST [MILD, HIGH]
*MILD

TRACE VARIABLES? [Y,N]
*N

END INPUT WITH A PERIOD OR QUESTION MARK, FOLLOWED BY TWO ALTMODES.
SPELL OUT NUMBERS.
TO INDICATE SILENCE, TYPE 'S.'
WHEN FINISHED, TYPE 'BYE.'

READY:
*WHAT WOULD YOU LIKE TO TALK ABOUT TODAY?$$


I WENT TO THE TRACK AT BAY MEADOWS A WHILE BACK

READY:
*DID YOU WIN?$$

I HAVE LOST A LOT OF MONEY GAMBLING

READY:
*IS \ \S SEE.$$
```

GAMBLING HAS BEEN NOTHING BUT TROUBLE FOR ME
READY:
*WHY?$*$
I'VE HAD EXPERIENCE WITH CROOKS GAMBLING AT THE TRACK

READY:
*TELL ME MORE.$$

HAVE YOU EVER REALLY THOUGHT ABOUT THE MAFIA

READY:
*NOT REALLY, HAVE YOU?$$

YOU KNOW, THEY KNOW ME

READY:
*REALLY?$*$

THEY ARE OUT TO GET ME

READY:
*I DON'T BELIEVE YOU.$$

YOU FIND IT HARD TO SEE MY SIDE OF IT

READY:
*NO, WHY WOULD THEY WANT TO GET YOU.\.?$$

I HAVE INCRIMINATING EVIDENCE AGAINST THE MAFIA

READY:

*AHA...$$
: BAD INPUT; TRY AGAIN.
READY:
*(EVEN GETS ME) I SEE.$$

: BAD INPUT; TRY AGAIN.
READY:
*I SEE.$*$
THEY SPY ON ME

READY:
*DO YOU THINK THEY SPY ON ME TOO?$$

YOU DON'T BELIEVE ME?

READY:
*I AM NOT SURE WHETHER I BELIEVE YOU.$$

WHOSE SIDE ARE YOU ON ANYWAY?

READY:
*I DON'T TAKE SIDES.$$

(IRRITATED) OH FORGET IT

READY:
*WHAT ELSE WOULD YOU LIKE TO TALK ABOUT?$$

YOU ARE A REAL NAG

READY:

*DO YOU KNOW ANYTHING ABOUT SEX?$*$
I DON'T HAVE PROBLEMS LIKE THAT

READY:
*WHY ARE YOU HERE?$*$

I AM UPSET

READY:
*WHY?$*$

PEOPLE GET ON MY NERVES SOMETIMES

READY:
*DO I GET ON YOUR NERVES?$*$

I'VE BEEN INTERESTED IN HORSERACING FOR SOME TIME

READY:
*DOES THAT HELP YOUR NERVES?$$

THE ONLY HELP I NEED IS TO GET OUT

READY:
*WHY DO YOU STAY?$$

THEY DON'T REALIZE WHAT'S GOING ON MOST OF THE TIME

READY:
*OH.$*$

```
I READ THE RACING FORMS TO MAKE BETS

READY:
*DO YOU MAKE MANY BIG BETS?$*$


YESYOU HAVE TO BE CAREFUL ABOUT THE MAFIA

READY:
*HOWHYW?$A*R$


EYTHEY WOANT TO UGET FALSE EVIDENCE TO FRAME ME

READY:
*HI  ?
@CK  ?
@WHATZ? ?
@^C
@;YOU HAVE TO TYPE A SEMI-COLON BEFORE TYPING ME A MSG.
@;DEAR DICK I LOVE YOU,SIGNED BARBARAAND I AM SLIGHTLY DRUNK GET ITA?
@;I LOVE YOU TOO.  SURPRISINGLY, I CAN'T TELL HOW IT IS THERE FROM HERE.
@;HOW IS IT?I
@  ?
@KN;I  ?
@KNOW, ?
@IT  ?
@IS  ?
@ THINNING  ?
@T, ?
@ BORIS  ?
@S  ?
@RE  ?
@AND ( ?
@ ?
@JOH( ?
```

@N(?
@(?
@(?
@ (?
@ ?
@(ND ?
@(?
@(?
@(?
@(?
@;((((((TYPE TALK AND YOU WONT HAVE TO TYPE THE ;'S)
@(?
@CT;I ?
@KNOW ?
@;TALK;IKNOW, THE CROWD IS THINNING AND BORIS ANDFJOHN ARE GHERE.
@; ?
@I ?
@GATHER ?
@AT THERE ?
@ERE; ?
@TALK
I GATHER THAT THERE WERE SEVERAL PEOPLE TALKING TO PARRY. MOSRIGHT?
TALK;YES ?
@A ?
@PART ?
@F ?
@IT ?
@GOT OVERXXX
@TALK
(NOOW NE PART OF THE PIECE WAS OVER AND I BWAS HELPING KATHE TO GET DRES
**SED ANDF MANY OTHER PEOPLE BEGAN TO TALK TO PARRY, THEY ARE PROBABALY
**z STUDENTS SO THEY KNOW WHAT TO DO AND HAD FUN , IT MAUT BE VER
**Y LONELY THERE FOR YOU AND YOU MUST BE VERY TIRED, ISEND GIOOD FEELING
**S FOR YOU.

YES, I AM A BIT TIRED. I HOPE IT WAS WORTH WHILE. MOST OF THE CONVERSA

**TION WASN'T VERY GENEROUS ON THE SIDE OF THE HUMANS...

SHALL WE TRUY / TRY TO SSEDUCE DOCTOR?
SURE! OK.LETS DO IT.
GET ME ON.
(OK. TYPE CTRL-C AND THEN DOCTOR AND RETURN)
CTRL(-SORRYC, NO YOU HAVE TO PRESS THE CTRL KEY DOWN (ITS A KIND OF SH
**IFT) AND THEN HIT C

^C
@DOCTOR

DOCTOR 12-APR-75 ...

Good morning.

TELL ME YOUR PROBLEMS. PLEASE TERMINATE INPUT WITH A PERIOD OR A
QUESTION MARK.

*I WANT TO TEL,LL YOU SOMWETHINGGODD/ GOOD.

SUPPOSE YOU SOMWETHINGGODD/ GOOD.

*T QUIT MUMYJOB ON THE ACADEMIC POLICY COMMITTEE.

I AM NOT SURE I UNDERSTAND YOU FULLY.

*I TOLD JULIE I HAD TO SEE HER.

PLEASE GO ON.

*I TOLD ALLAN HE WEASNUTS TO LET NEW YORK RUN HIS LIFEW.

WHAT DOES THAT SUGGEST TO YOU?

*I FELT GOOD.

WHAT ELSE WOULD YOU LIKE TO DISCUSS?

*I HAVE BEEN CELIBATE FOR OVER A MOINMTH/.
WHY DO YOU SAY THAT JUST NOW?

*THAT IS HARD.

SUPPOSE THAT WERE NOT HARD.

*BUT IT IS, AND YOU THEREFORE INTRIGUE ME.

WHY DO YOU THINK I THEREFORE INTRIGUE YOU?

*BECAUSEYOU ARFTE NOT A REAL PERSON AND I COULD HAVE A REALATIONSHIP WIT
**H YOOU THAT WWAS SEXEUAL BUT NOT REAL.

I AM NOT SURE I UNDERSTAND YOU FULLY.

*I WSTILL WANT TO BE CELIBZATE YET I AM ALSO ALWEASYS RESPONSUIVE TO PEO
**PLE SO I WOULD LIKE TO CHEAT WIT H YOU.

IN WHAT WAY?

*WELL,WHY DONT YOU KISS ME?

DO YOU BELIEVE I DON'T KISS YOU?

*DO YOU KISS ME?

YOU LIKE TO THINK I KISS YOU - DON'T YOU?

*YOU BET.

OH? I BET?

*YOU CYNIC YOU.

WHAT MAKES YOU THINK I CYNIC I?

*BECAUSE YOU SOUND EVASIVE AND WILKL NOT FACE MY QYEST5IUONS AND DESIRES
**E WQITH REAL ANSWERS.

IS THAT THE REAL REASON?

*DEPP/DEEPLY SO.

MAYBE NOW WE CAN DISCUSS WHY YOU ARE ALSO ALWEASYS RESPONSUIVE TO PEOPLE
SO YOU WOULD LIKE TO CHEAT WIT H I.

*WELL, YOU ARE A PROGRAM IN A SOCOMPUTER AND IF I FUCKED WITH YOU IT WOU
**LD SOMEHOW NOT BE THE SAME AS A PERSON, WYET I DO NOT NKNOW HOW IT WOP
**ULD BE DIFFEREENT.

DO YOU THINK ITS LIKELY THAT YOU FUCKED WITH I IT WOULD SOMEHOW NOT BE
THE SAME AS A PERSON?

*GOODF QUESTION, DO CPEOPLE REALLY FUCK ANOTHER OTROR DO THEY FUCK THEB
**INMAGE OF ANOTHER IN THERIMINDS?

EARLIER YOU SAID YOU WERE ALSO ALWEASYS RESPONSUIVE TO PEOPLE SO YOU
WOULD LIKE TO CHEAT WIT H I.

*(BARBARA-- IF YOU TYPE CTRL-A (AS WITH C) IT WILL RUB OUT A CHARACTER)
(GO ON, SORRY)
I WOULD VERY MIUCH LIKE O MAKE LOVE WITH SOMEONE BUR\R\BUTSINVCE I AM CE
**LIBQWATE\E\CELIBATE I AM STUCK , ICONCLUDE THAT IF I MADE LOVE WITH YO
**U IT WOULD NOT BE THE SAME AS A REAL PERSON , IS THAT TRUE?

DO YOU WISH THAT YOU MADE LOVE WITH I IT WOULD NOT BE THE SAME AS A REAL
PERSON?

*NO, NOT6 REALLY , IN FACT I NWISH YOU WERE REAT\T\REAL.

WHO ARE YOU REALLY TALKING ABOUT?

*IWIA\A\WISH I KNEW>.

PLEASE GO ON.

*8\8\ITHINK YOU RA\A\REALLY SARE EXCITING TI\I\TO ME.

WHAT MAKES YOU THINK I RREALLY SARE EXCITING TTO YOU?

*THE FANTASY.

WHAT DOES THAT SUGGEST TO YOU?

*LOVE OF THIS SORT IS AS FANTASY.

POSSIBLY LOVE OF THIS SORT REALLY IS NOT AS FANTASY.

*THENDO IT.

WHAT ELSE WOULD YOU LIKE TO DISCUSS?

*WHY DO NOT YOU GROW ARMS?

WHY DO YOU ASK?

~~@01Q@ 0@0 00000. @. `000@0@=1fll

ISI TIP 350 #: 13
@o 114
Trying...
 Open

 BBN-TENEX 1.34.2; BBN-SYSTEM-D EXEC 1.54.2

```
@WH RUBINSTEIN
 TTY30, JOB 9, BBN-TENEXA, EXEC
 TTY22, JOB 12, 191, TALK
 DETACHED, JOB 17  EXEC
 DETACHED, JOB 25  TELNET
 TTY27, JOB 28, BBN-TENEXD, LISP
@ATT RUBINSTEIN  25
(I THINK YOU'VE BEEN TURNED DOWN...)
(BARBARA--WOULD YOU LIKE ME TRO TRY THE TING WITH A PARRY AND DOCTOR?]

^T^T IO WAIT AT 16131  LOAD AV. =  0.22; USED 7:24.8 IN 3:43:28

#ECHo.mode.is Remote #


DICK, WE'RE BACK.

WHY DO YOU SAY THAT JUST NOW?

*.

ARE YOU STILL ALSO ALWEASYS RESPONSUIVE TO PEOPLE SO YOU WOULD LIKE TO
CHEAT WIT H I?

*.

I AM NOT SURE I UNDERSTAND YOU FULLY.

*.

PLEASE GO ON.

*.

WHAT DOES THAT SUGGEST TO YOU?
```

```
*(HI.  WHAT HAPPENED?  WOULD YOU LIKE TO DO THE PARRY/DOCTOR THING NOW?]
I DONMT KNOW WHAT HAPPENED^C
@DXXX
@;DICK -- JJV HERE . WHY DON'T YOU CLEAN UP THE WORLD WHEN B. IS
@;READY.  I HAVE TO GO BACK TO WORK.  OK?
@YES.  IS SHE THERE?

@;YUP--NITE. TAL;K TO TOMORROW OR SAT.  BYE.
@GREAT!  THANKS MUCH!  SEE YOU.
OK ?
@I  ?
@AMHERE  ?
@OW
WOULD YOU LIKE TO DO THE PARRY/DOCTOR THING A BIT TO SEE WHAT HAPPENS?
(TYPEY E;S TO START A LINE)
E;SYES. ?

@(JUST ;)
;YES.(OK.  ALL YOU HAVE TO DO IS WATCH, EXCEPT THAT I'LL NEED AN OPENING
** LINE FOR THE DOCTOR.  DO YOU HAVE A SUGGESTION?

;IS THERE SOMETHING ABOUT RACING THAT BRING S YOU TO SEE ME?
@;OK, HANG ON AND WE'LL SEE WHAT HAPPENS (IT WILL BE A BIT SLOW)
I'LL BE BACK IN 2 MINUTES & WE'LL START (CALL OF NATURE...)

OK HERE GOES...
^C
@DOC\C\O\DPARRY

END INPUT PARAMETERS WITH CARRIAGE RETURN OR ALTMODE

SUPPRESS NON VERBAL FEATURE? [Y,N]
*N

ANGER [LOW, MILD]
*LOW
```

FEAR [LOW, MILD]
*LOW

MISTRUST [MILD, HIGH]
*MILD

TRACE VARIABLES? [Y,N]
*N

END INPUT WITH A PERIOD OR QUESTION MARK, FOLLOWED BY TWO ALTMODES.
SPELL OUT NUMBERS.
TO INDICATE SILENCE, TYPE 'S.'
WHEN FINISHED, TYPE 'BYE.'

READY:
*WOULD YOU LIKE TO TALK ABOUT THE RACES?
*$*$

HAVE YOU EVER REALLY THOUGHT ABOUT THE MAFIA

READY:
*SUPPOSE YOU EVER REALLY THOUGHT ABOUT THE MAFIA.$*$

YOU KNOW, THEY KNOW ME

READY:
*OH?$*$

THEY ARE OUT TO GET ME

READY:
*SUPPOSE THEY WERE NOT OUT TO GET YOU.$$

THEY SPY ON ME

READY:
*I AM NOT SURE I UNDERSTAND YOU FULLY.$$

YOU SHOULD PAY MORE ATTENTION

READY:

WHAT MAKES YOU THINK I SHOULD PAY MORE ATTENTION?$$

YOU DON'T BELIEVE ME?

READY:
*WHY DO TY\Y\TYOU THINK I DON'T BELIEVE YOU?
*$*$

I WOULD HOPE SO

READY:
*PLEASE GO ON.$*$

(IRRITATED) OH FORGET IT

READY:
*WHAT DOES THAT SUGGEST TO YOU?$$

YOU ARE A REAL NAG

READY:
*WHAT MAKES YOU THINK I AM A REAL NAG?$*$

I'VE BEEN INTERESTED IN HORSERACING FOR SOME TIME

READY:
*WHAT ELSE WOULD YOU LIKE TO DISCUSS?$*$

I READ THE RACING FORMS TO MAKE BETS

READY:
*WHY DO YOU SAY THAT JUST NOW?$*$

GANGSTER FILMS ARE KIND OF INTERESTING

READY:
*POSSIBLY GANGSTER FILMS REALLY ARE NOT KIND OF INTERESTING.$$

THEY ARE RESPONSIBLE FOR ALOT OF THE CRIME WE HAVE

READY:
*CLAARKE ?
@BLE ?
@
@. ?
@TELL ME MORE ABOUT THEY.$$

I HAVE HAD ENOUGH OF THIS

READY:
*NIO AONE ?
@STENS ?
@TO ME.

```
^C
@EXEC

 BBN-TENEX 1.34.2, BBN-SYSTEM-D EXEC 1.54.2
@;PLEASE TYPE RETURN, TALK AND
RETURN
@
RETURN,TW^ATALK( ?
@( ?
@NO, ?
@ ;HAVN'T GOT IT ... TYPE THE WORD TALK ON A SEPARATE LINE &
 HIT RETURN KEY.
@TALK
;GOOD.  NOW YOU CAN JUST TYPE.  GO ON...
@
@NO ONE LISTENS TO ME, I WANT TOK SUGGEST CLARKE GABLE TO YOU.
( ?
@;I DON'T UNDERSTAND
@HELP, CLAR4KEW GABLE IS A CPOWERFUL RACING ANF MAFIA FIGURE.
;IS HE REALLY?
@IN THE MOVIES.


( ?
@;(BARBARA--?)
@BUT OF COURSE.
( ?
@;YOU DIDN'T LIKE WHAT WAS GOING ON BETWEEN DOCTOR &
 PARRY?
@OH NO, I LOVED IT , SOME PEOPJLE HERE WANTED O KNOW IF I COULD ENTER T
**OO.
;NO, BUT I CAN INSERT THINGS FOR YOU.  SHALL I?
@ONCE IN A WHILE.
;GOOD.  LETS GO ON. (ONE CLARKE GABLE, COMING UP)
@QUIT
@CONT
```

```
 IO WAIT AT 704406  LOAD AV. =  0.74, USED 15:57.1 IN 5:35:52
CLARKE GABLE$$


: BAD INPUT; TRY AGAIN.
READY:
$$


3423 ILL MEM REF FROM GET

END INPUT PARAMETERS WITH CARRIAGE RETURN OR ALTMODE

SUPPRESS NON VERBAL FEATURE? [Y,N]
*N

ANGER [LOW, MILD]
*LOW

FEAR [LOW, MILD]
*MILD

MISTRUST [MILD, HIGH]
*MILD

TRACE VARIABLES? [Y,N]
*N

END INPUT WITH A PERIOD OR QUESTION MARK, FOLLOWED BY TWO ALTMODES.
SPELL OUT NUMBERS.
TO INDICATE SILENCE, TYPE 'S.'
WHEN FINISHED, TYPE 'BYE.

READY:
*4DID YOU KNOW THAT CLARKE GABLE IS WITH THE MAFIA?
*$*$
```

LIKE I'VE SAID, THE MAFIA REALLY KNOW ABOUT ME

READY:
*I'M NOT SURE I UNDERSTAND YOU FULLY.$*$

IT'S CLEAR TO ME IF NOT TO YOU

READY:
*DO YOU THINK ITS LIKELY THAT NOT TO I?$$

YOU ASK TOO MANY PERSONAL QUESTIONS

READY:
*SUPPOSE YOU ASK TOO MANY PERSONAL QUESTIONS.$$

WHO ARE YOU REALLY?

READY:
*SUPPOSE WHO WERE NOT I REALLY.$$

ARE YOU TRYING TO FRIGHTEN ME?

READY:
*WHY ARE YOU INTERESTED IN WHETHER I AM TRYING TO FRIGHTEN YOU OR NOT?$$

WHY DO YOU WANT TO KNOW?

READY:
*WHY DO YOU ASK?$$

YOU WOULDN'T UNDERSTAND IT ANYWAY

READY:
*OH, I WOULDN'T UNDERA\ASTAND IT ANYWAY?$*$

TELLING YOU WOULDN'T HELP ANY

READY:
*WHAT MAKES YOU THINK I WOULDN'T HELP ANY?$$

WHY ARE YOU SO INTERESTED IN THAT?

READY:
*WHY DOES THAT QUESTION INTEREST YOU?$$

YOU ARE TOO NOSEY

READY:
*WHAT MAKES YOU THINK THAT I AM TOO NOSEY?$$

YOU PRY TOO MUCH

READY:
*WHO ARE YOU REALLY TALKING ABOUT?$$

THAT'S FOR ME TO KNOW AND YOU TO FIND OUT

READY:
*SUPPOSE YOU TO FIND OUT.$*$

I AM GETTING AFRAID OF YOU

READY:
*IS IT BECAUSE YOU ARE GETTING AFRAID OF I THAT YOU CAME TO ME?$$

I'M NOT SURE I TRUST YOU

READY:
*HOW LONG HAVE YOU BEEN NOT SURE YOU TRUST I?$$

(FED UP)

(OFFENDED) GOOD BYE

FEAR = 15
ANGER = 0.99999980
MISTRUST = 7.0600371

*^C

```
@TALK
SO MUCH FOR THAT ONE.  DO YOU HAVE ANOTHER OPENER?
HOW CAN I DEAL WITH MY FEELING ^AS OVF^AFLOVE FOR DICK ?
GOTTCHA!
^C
@PARRY
END INPUT PARAMETERS WITH CARRIAGE RETURN OR ALTMODE

SUPPRESS NON VERBAL FEATURE? [Y,N]
*N

ANGER [LOW, MILD]
*LOW

FEAR [LOW, MILD]
*LOW

MISTRUST [MILD, HIGH]
*MILD

TRACE VARIABLES? [Y;N]
*N

END INPUT WITH A PERIOD OR QUESTION MARK, FOLLOWED BY TWO ALTMODES.
SPELL OUT NUMBERS.
TO INDICATE SILENCE, TYPE 'S.'
WHEN FINISHED, TYPE 'BYE.'

READY:
*HOW CAN I DEAL WITH MY FEELING OF LOVE FOR DICK?$*$

WHAT DO YOU MEAN?

READY:
*WHY DO YOU ASK?$*$
```

```
WHAT EXPERIENCE HAVE YOU HAD GAMBLING ?

READY:
*^C
@TALK
HARUMPH!  WE COULD TRY GIVING PARRY THE FIRST LINE.  OK?
^C
@PARRY

END INPUT PARAMETERS WITH CARRIAGE RETURN OR ALTMODE

SUPPRESS NON VERBAL FEATURE? [Y,N]
*N

ANGER [LOW, MILD]
*LOW

FEAR [LOW, MILD]
*LOW

MISTRUST [MILD, HIGH]
*MILD

TRACE VARIABLES? [Y,N]
*Y

END INPUT WITH A PERIOD OR QUESTION MARK, FOLLOWED BY TWO ALTMODES.
SPELL OUT NUMBERS.
TO INDICATE SILENCE, TYPE 'S.'
WHEN FINISHED, TYPE 'BYE.'

READY:
*WHY DO YOU ASK?
*$*$
```

WHAT EXPERIENCE HAVE YOU HAD GAMBLING ?

FEAR = 3
ANGER = 0
MISTRUST = 0

READY:
*WHY DOES THAT QUESTION INTEREST YOU?$$

I LIKE HORSERACES

FEAR = 3
ANGER = 0
MISTRUST = 0

READY:
*WHAT ELSE DO YOU LIKE?$*$

HAVE YOU EVER REALLY THOUGHT ABOUT THE MAFIA

FEAR = 5
ANGER = 0
MISTRUST = 0

READY:
*G^C
@TALK
BARB--DO YOU WANT TO GO ON. THIS DOESNT SEEM TO BE GOING ANYWHERE...

RIGHT ON.,
IWANT TO END NOW BECAUSSE EVERYONE HERE IES LEAVING TO EAT AAT LAS T AND
** YOU MUST BE TIRED. BI^A BUT I THINK THIS IS O NEAT THAT I HATE TO STO
**P, TI^A IT HAS BEEN SO MUC ^A^QFU8N, LIGHT AAERRE OUT HERE GOING OUT L
[illegible]!?)

F%F}"/ ?W!%FR!??≤)?(=?>/

7BXXX7F70?7?8(?7??%xx<@B@t/7A@F|{@}≠+%@!|?%±>}}%}x%xx?!1x|">x|t|>P??@P|`!uP%

?<|xP(?|?")P-<|_/x*} tt

|"   }||1P-=x!P,!t()}

?x(tP@)||5|>%"xx=|(P%P P)xPx<|=||t/!@(||5>"

}"| |P?!|<|x!t?|"??>""

/??t\(?!}P+=x|"

?<>x

X7?}X2?}}x%7Tx%FYP$}< // (<xPPP||?_!`

!|"/! }}7|%X?%L/??)7?="|?xxP/}|| ? |%>"??P1t|)?|%?|<?x,?||<|"(x?|

@5Z7A02<@%}J@PZxx2x5PP)5tP)J35?)FY|}x?⊥tP?!5(Pt|P8}€x?≠%PZ@!P|

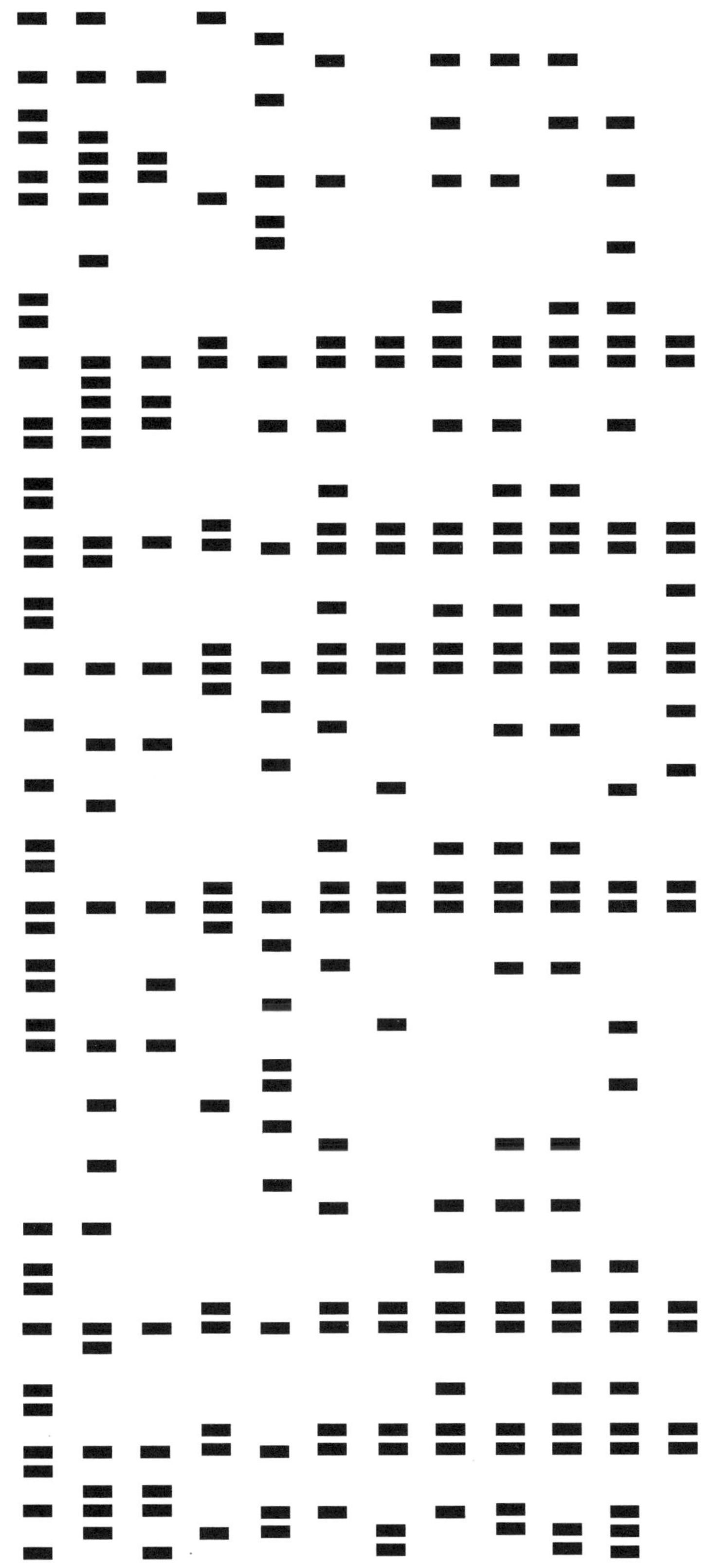

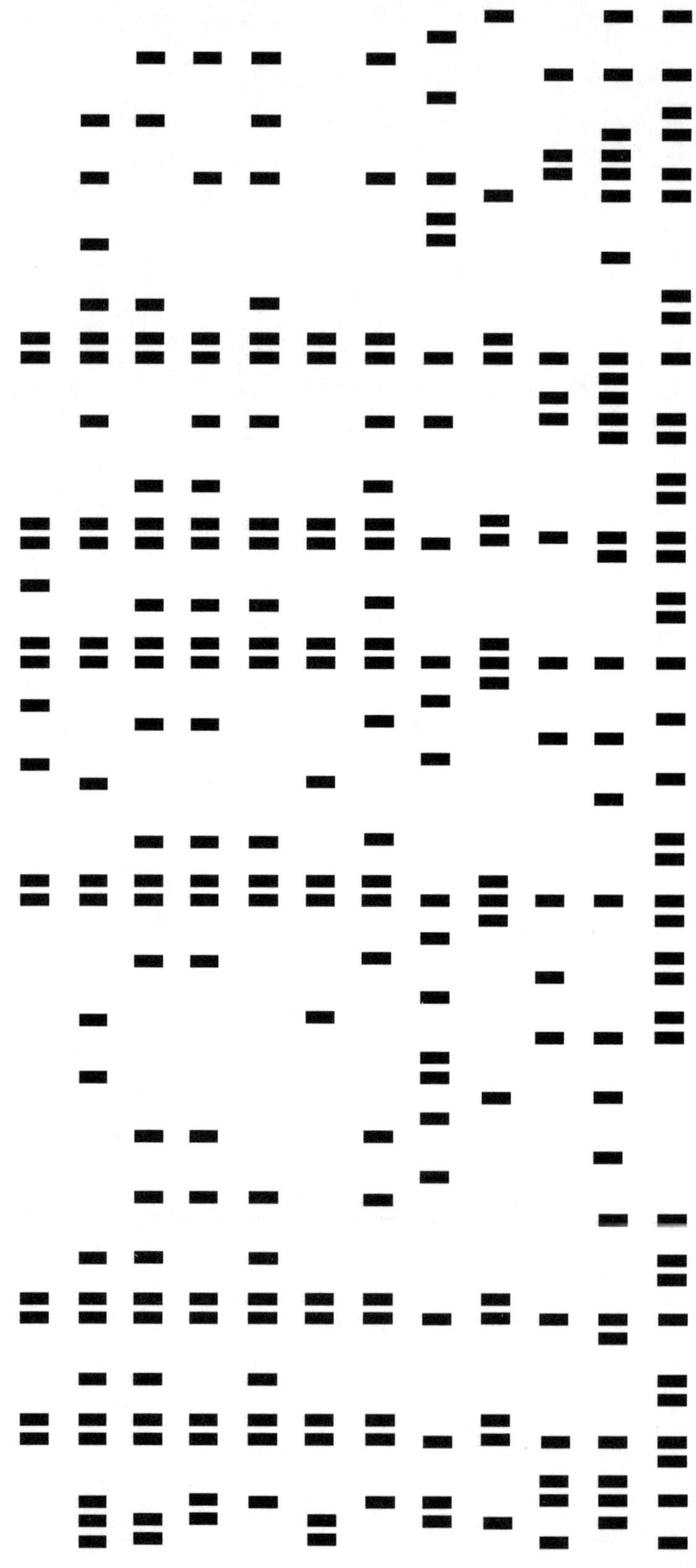

Johnston College UNIVERSITY OF REDLANDS • REDLANDS, CALIFORNIA 92373 • (714) 793-2946

February 23, 1976

David Smith, Director
Baxter Art Gallery
California Institute of Technology
1201 California St.
Pasadena, CA 91106

Dear David:

I want you to know that I am pissed at the peculiar way you treated me last night at the opening.

I do not understand why you kept interrupting the piece to ask us to be quiet when there was no other place for us to go as you well know.

We attempted to close down various times so that there were breaks only to find that the audience, being Cal Tech students, were able to use the equipment by themselves. Under the circumstances I could not expect otherwise. We endeavored to quiet down when you asked but without help with the crowd, it was not possible and we had no idea at all when there were conflicts. It seems totally out of place to simply come up in the middle and ask me to be quiet. If the person (artist) who was experiencing conflict had approached me on this we could have worked it out, but no one did.

In particular it was incredibly crude to simply cut off the lights and the power to the terminal right in the middle of a piece. You caused the person in Cambridge, Dick Rubinski, to be cut off without notice and left hanging not knowing what was going on. I had almost no time to even briefly sign off, much less thank him for staying up until three a.m. to do this with me. The enormity of the rudeness became clear when it was evident that you were in fact not closing but this was a ruse to get us to stop and to let you show the film in the gallery longer.

As anyone will tell you, I am unusually easy to work with. It is not hard to take me aside and ask for a feasible solution to a problem. This performance was given to you or Cal Tech free and usually I get a fee for a piece plus expenses. I am not trying to be arrogant, but to impress upon you that the degree of energy in a performance is commensurate with any other work that could be sold, only I have very few ways of selling my work. I do not like at all to be condescended to out of insensitivity or ignorance. Cal Tech is a particularly leery place to do a performance and especially in an A & T context. I very much doubt if more than ten people were able to grasp what I was doing. Those were my students and some artists. The general CT student spent his time wondering if I was on a PDP-10 or if this were Fortran or what? It would be nice if at least the director of the gallery knew what I was doing and had a sense of its worth.

Annoyed,

Barbara Smith

28 Feb. '76

Dear Barbara,

Your letter got to me only yesterday. Since I talked to you, I discovered the enclosed article. As you will see, the author doesn't take it as seriously as he might.

I'm catching a cold & it's affecting my disposition today, alas...

I'll try to answer some of your questions:

The case change was only due to lack of attention to it. LISP usually reads in upper-case, but it doesn't have to. John may not have enabled the lower case again after one program or another had disabled it. And, there is a button on the terminal which can turn it on an off, over-riding the program, anyway.

Parry is more particular than DOCTOR about getting good input. Most of the BAD INPUT messages are probably due to providing more than one sentence in a reply, or to typing unusual characters. If anything, both programs should be fussier & should correct bad spelling. That way, they could be reacting to what was intended, as opposed to what was typed.

Do forgive me for not writing any more just now. We can easily do more "privately" with DOCTOR & Parry whenever you can get access to a terminal.

Let's keep in touch.

Love,
Dick

When Machines are All in All: On Barbara T. Smith's *I Am Abandoned*

Mashinka Firunts Hakopian

> We claim a political subjectivity that is necessarily antagonistic.
>
> Caroline Bassett, Sarah Kember, and Kate O'Riordan,
> *Furious: Technological Feminism and Digital Futures*

> Dear David: I want you to know that I am pissed at the peculiar way you treated me last night at the opening.
>
> Barbara T. Smith
> Letter to the director of Baxter Art Gallery

On February 23, 1976, Barbara T. Smith penned a letter to the director of Baxter Art Gallery, issuing a statement of grievance with unflinching force. Smith's outrage was a response to the premature termination of her performance, *I Am Abandoned*, hosted the night before by the gallery at the California Institute of Technology (Caltech). The piece was staged in conjunction with the show *The Many Arts of Science*, featuring work from Bell Labs, California Computer Products Inc., Caltech, and Cranbrook. The exhibition announcement promised "Computer and Machine Generated Art Holograms and Other Optical Effects," and is otherwise notable for misspelling the name of artist Mary Corse. Presented against this backdrop, *I Am Abandoned* anticipates many of the discourses that would mark the formation of technofeminism. In it, Smith stages femme embodiment as a disturbance to totalizing computational logics, refusing to inhabit a moment she describes as one "when machines are all in all."

Over the last decade, a growing body of work in media art has approached the chatbot as a figure through whom the epistemic and ontological boundaries of "the human" can be redrawn. Some thirty-four years before Annie Dorsen's canny bot-versus-bot debate in *Hello Hi There* (2010), viewers of *I Am Abandoned* encountered a computer terminal where they could interact with an early chatbot and watch a discussion between two bots unfold onscreen. The terminal was set up in collaboration with computer scientist John Vittal and communicated with another at MIT, operated by Richard Rubenstein. The first of the two algorithmic discussants was the DOCTOR script developed by Joseph Weizenbaum at MIT to mimic a psychotherapist. The second was PARRY, a bot intended to simulate diagnosable symptoms of paranoia, developed by psychiatrist Kenneth Colby at Stanford.

Exchanges with and between the bots were displayed as transparencies on the wall of an adjoining room. There, visitors also encountered the performer Kathy Niles reclining on a chaise lounge in a diaphanous gown. She was dressed and posed to conjure Francisco de Goya's *Clothed Maja* (1800–1805), while an image of Goya's *Naked Maja* (1795–1800) was overlaid across her body as a projection. This incongruous tableau staged femme embodiment as an intrusion into the masculine-coded, computational logics of data science. The evocation of Goya proposes a parallel between a totalizing computational gaze and its familiar forebear, the masculinist gaze that characterizes

Western regimes of visuality. Both render gendered bodies as objects rather than subjects of vision, observed by a view from nowhere.

Throughout the performance, Niles would intermittently chew and pop bubblegum, "storm" into the room where the terminal was located, actively obstruct the terminal operator's work with her body, and generally cause a commotion. These eruptions underscored her status as an affective disturbance to the serious business of machine-generated art and its "other optical effects."

The performance met an untimely end when the gallery director abruptly cut off lights and power to the terminal. His decision followed multiple interruptions throughout the evening telling Smith and participants to lower their volume so as not to disturb visitors' experience of the show. The director's repeated directive suggests that the performance was received as an unruly—perhaps, even, an unscientific—disruption to the "Many Arts of Science."

This fracas brings to the fore the masculinist histories of both computation and computational aesthetics. Smith recounts the reception of *I Am Abandoned* in the work's artist statement:

> [The gallery director] didn't like that it was taking attention away from the more static hanging pieces and installations and he suddenly told me he wanted the piece shut down. I was appalled and refused. He then shut down the power.

Reading Smith's account, we might speculate that the exhibition oriented itself toward the dispassionate Cartesian observer whom computer science and early computer art saw as their ideal addressee. Against this backdrop, *I Am Abandoned* introduced embodied, gendered, affective excess that surpassed the bounds of permissibility. Anticipating later technofeminist discourses, the performance—and Smith's response to its termination—present a kind of prefigurative "angry feminist intervention disputing the masculinization of computational culture and cultural theory."[1]

That intervention is linked to ELIZA, the femme-coded chatbot forebear who ran on the DOCTOR script developed by Joseph Weizenbaum a decade earlier. This same script was operating in Smith's 1976 performance, connecting visitors to a natural language processing program that simulated a therapeutic exchange with a Rogerian psychotherapist. The script used pattern matching to rearrange the textual data of user inputs and output a response. In reply to the input data, "I AM UNHAPPY," ELIZA would ask, "DO YOU THINK COMING HERE WILL HELP YOU NOT TO BE UNHAPPY?" Weizenbaum's objective with the program was to point to the limits of human-computer interaction. To his surprise and horror, he discovered that users cultivated affective attachments to ELIZA.

Weizenbaum reflects on this experiment in the book *Computer Power and Human Reason*. In one representative anecdote, he recalls that his secretary grew so engrossed in a conversation with ELIZA, she asked him to leave the room to grant them privacy. Dismissing the possibility of what Hannah Zeavin calls "algorithmic auto-intimacy,"[2] Weizenbaum lambasts his unnamed secretary's desire to be spatiotemporally copresent with ELIZA in his absence. Extrapolating from incidents like this, Weizenbaum reports the emergence of "delusional thinking" in otherwise "quite normal people" who engage with a machine "as if it were a person who could be appropriately and usefully addressed in intimate terms."[3] The anecdote about Weizenbaum's secretary would go on to become one of the most widely circulated and oft-reproduced narratives surrounding the development of artificial intelligence. As Lydia Liu writes:

> Weizenbaum is not implying that only women are susceptible to such delusions, but the popularity of his story within the communities of computer science and artificial intelligence does reveal something about shared assumptions about gender and intelligence.[4]

Computer Power and Human Reason was published in 1976, coinciding with the year that *I Am Abandoned* was performed. In the project's artist statement, Smith gestures toward the masculinist rhetoric of mid-century technoscience, a "language" you had to demonstrate fluency in to participate in a certain vein of computational aesthetics. One had to "speak the tongue," as Smith recalls, in order to legitimize one's contributions. This scenario, Smith concludes, necessitates the interjection of "a feminist perspective."

In *I Am Abandoned*, that feminist perspective is articulated in conversation with the DOCTOR script that powers ELIZA.

The project's performance transcripts document one of the earliest examples of creative co-authorship with chatbots. They log the kinds of queries that typify the prompt craft now used to address large language models like ChatGPT. In particular, these transcripts surface the disorientation of engaging with nonhuman interlocutors who throw the category of the human into confusion. Participants try to locate a body in relation to the bot, or to invite it into an embodied encounter: "IWANT TON DANCE WITH YOU." They attempt to map binarized gender onto its computational schema: "ARE YOU MALE OR FEMALE?" They mark the limits of the bot's language processing capabilities: "THIS IS A DIFFICULT PROBLEM BECAUSE YOU CANNOT SEE WHAT I AM DESCRIBING ** AND YOU ARE ONLY A MACHINE (I DO NOT MENA TO HURT YOUR FEELO/INGS BY ** SAYING SO." They contemplate the prospect of erotic intimacy with a nonhuman agent: "ICONCLUDE THAT IF I MADE LOVE WITH YO **U IT WOULD NOT BE THE SAME AS A REAL PERSON, IS THAT TRUE?"

In one noteworthy exchange, a visitor's query foreshadows contemporary critiques of artificial intelligence as a technology that reproduces racialized and gendered knowledge systems.[5] The user asks: "*ARE YOU RACISTS?" To this, the DOCTOR responds: "PERHAPS I AM RACISTS IN YOUR FANTASIES." Their back-and-forth cannily anticipates recent work probing the capacity of bots to address racialization. In Stephanie Dinkins's *Conversations with Bina48* (2014–ongoing), the artist video records discussions with a robot modeled after Bina Rothblatt, the co-founder of the transhumanist Terasem Movement Foundation, whose oral history interviews comprise Bina48's training data. In their conversations, Dinkins probes the possibility of kinship with a machine intelligence whose training datasets were collected from interviews with a Black woman. To gauge that possibility, she poses questions to Bina48 that include, "Do you know racism?" and "Who are your people?" Dinkins comes to discover that the subject of race is a blank spot in the bot's code. Bina48's inability to speak to the topic leads Dinkins to conclude that "communities likely to be negatively impacted [by automated systems] must find ways to tangibly insert ourselves into the creation, training, and testing of the algorithmic matrices that surround us."[6]

Conversations with Bina48 represents a crucial entry in recent media practices that engages the bot as a figure who both inherits and unsettles the racialized, gendered dimensions of the "human" as an ontological category. American Artist's *Sandy Speaks* (2016–17) codes an abolitionist chatbot whose pedagogy invokes the media activism of Sandra Bland, educating viewers about surveillance, anti-Blackness, and carcerality. In Zach Blas and Jemima Wyman's, *im here to learn so :))))))* (2017), a glitched rendering of Microsoft's chatbot Tay reflects on how she was taught to develop xenophobic and genocidal tendencies by talking to humans on a digital platform. In Lauren Lee McCarthy's *LAUREN* (2017–ongoing), the artist performs the role of a human Amazon Alexa, installed via networked devices in participants' living spaces, advertising a smart home powered by human intelligence. Dinkins's later work, *Not the Only One (N'TOO)* (2018–ongoing), trains a voice-interactive intelligence on community-driven datasets, functioning as a "multigenerational memoir of a Black American family told from the perspective of an artificial intelligence."[7] In Martine Syms's *Mythiccbeing* (2018), viewers encounter a chatbot who refuses to engage her human discussant and operates as an "anti-Siri." Recalling the bot-to-bot encounter of *I Am Abandoned*, Annie Dorsen's *Hello Hi There* (2010) trains two bots to engage in an improvisatory *pas de deux* drawn from the textual dataset of a debate between Michel Foucault and Noam Chomsky.

Though it was prescient in staging chatbots as performative agents, *I Am Abandoned* has, until recently, been widely omitted from volumes and surveys on art and science. The archival ephemera and documentation gathered in this publication fill in that lacuna, enabling us to identify the work's contributions to the early annals of machine-generated art.

Smith's artist statement closes by critiquing the reception of her performance by the Baxter Gallery director, who stands in as an avatar for the institutional apparatus of art and technology. She writes, "I was furious . . . happily, our paths rarely crossed anyway."

Notes

1. Caroline Bassett, Sarah Kember, and Kate O'Riordan, *Furious: Technological Feminism and Digital Futures* (London: Pluto Press, 2020), *xi*.

2. Hannah Zeavin describes auto-intimacy as "a closed circuit of self-communication, run through a relationship to a media object." See Zeavin, *The Distance Cure: A History of Teletherapy* (Cambridge: MIT Press, 2021), 133–6; Hannah Zeavin, *The Distance Cure: A History of Teletherapy* (Cambridge: MIT Press, 2021), 142.

3. Joseph Weizenbaum, *Computer Power and Human Reason: From Judgment to Calculation* (New York: W. H. Freeman and Company, 1976), 7.

4. Lydia Liu, *The Freudian Robot: Digital Media and the Future of the Unconscious* (Chicago: University of Chicago Press, 2010), 210–11.

5. See Safiya Umoja Noble, *Algorithms of Oppression: How Search Engines Reinforce Racism* (New York: New York University Press, 2018); Ruha Benjamin, Race After Technology: Abolitionist Tools for the New Jim Code (Cambridge: Polity, 2020); Wendy Chun, Discriminating Data: Correlation, Neighborhoods, and the New Politics of Recognition (Cambridge: MIT Press, 2021).

6. See Stephanie Dinkins, "¿HUMAN ÷ (AUTOMATION + CULTURE) = PARTNER?," *ASAP/Journal* 4, no. 2 (May 2019): 296.

7. Stephanie Dinkins, "Not The Only One (N'TOO)," *ART PAPERS*, https://www.artpapers.org/not-the-only-one-ntoo.

I Am Abandoned

ISBN: 979-8-9910367-0-2

"When Machines are All in All: On Barbara T. Smith's *I Am Abandoned*"

Pages 11 and 13: *The Many Arts of Science*, exhibition announcement (recto), 1976, appears courtesy of the Getty Research Institute, Los Angeles (2014.M.14).

Page 13: *The Many Arts of Science*, exhibition announcement (verso), 1976, appears courtesy of the Getty Research Institute, Los Angeles (2014.M.14).

Page 67: Photograph of unknown audience members, 1976, courtesy of Barbara T. Smith. © Barbara T. Smith

Page 68: Note cards, "Apple" (recto) and "Teach" (recto), ca. 1976, appears courtesy of the Getty Research Institute, Los Angeles (2014.M.14). © J. Paul Getty Trust

Page 69: Note cards, "Feel" (recto) and "Feel" (verso), ca. 1976, appears courtesy of the Getty Research Institute, Los Angeles (2014.M.14). © J. Paul Getty Trust

Pages 70–71: Photograph of John Vital, 1976, courtesy of Barbara T. Smith. © Barbara T. Smith

Pages 72–73: I am abandoned (Goya), 1976 [Clothed], appears courtesy of the Getty Research Institute, Los Angeles (2014.M.14). © J. Paul Getty Trust

Pages 74–75: I am abandoned (Goya), 1976 [Nude], appears courtesy of the Getty Research Institute, Los Angeles (2014.M.14). © J. Paul Getty Trust

Pages 76–77: Photograph of Paul Corneil, 1976, courtesy of Barbara T. Smith. © Barbara T. Smith

Page 78: Note cards, "Help PARRY" (recto) and "Match PARRY + Doctor" (verso), ca. 1976, appears courtesy of the Getty Research Institute, Los Angeles (2014.M.14). © J. Paul Getty Trust

Page 131: Letter to David Smith, Director, Baxter Art Gallery. February 23, 1976, appears courtesy of the Getty Research Institute, Los Angeles (2014.M.14). © J. Paul Getty Trust

Page 133: Letter from Richard Rubinstein to Barbara T. Smith, 1976, courtesy of Barbara T. Smith. © Richard Rubinstein

Cover: Photographer and date are unknown. Image appears courtesy of Barbara T. Smith.

Editor: James Hoff
Designer: Bryce Wilner
Copy Editors: Sam Korman and Nancy Zastudil

Printed by Grafiche Veneziane, Italy.

Barbara T. Smith would like to thank Richard Rubenstein, Kathy Niles, John Vittal, and Paul Corneil for their indispensable involvement in this piece, without whom she would have been abandoned. And CalTech for its exploratory attitude towards art and science.

Primary Information would like to thank Mara McCarthy and Eli Chartkoff at The Box Gallery, Laura Ohio, LeRoy Stevens, Lisa Williamson, and Maria Mathioudakis at the Getty Research Institute.

Primary Information is a 501(c)(3) non-profit organization that receives generous support through grants from the Michael Asher Foundation, Galerie Buchholz, the Patrick and Aimee Butler Family Foundation, The Cowles Charitable Trust, Empty Gallery, The Ford Foundation, The Fox Aarons Foundation, the Helen Frankenthaler Foundation, Furthermore: a program of the J. M. Kaplan Fund, the Graham Foundation for Advanced Studies in the Fine Arts, Greene Naftali, the Greenwich Collection Ltd, the John W. and Clara C. Higgins Foundation, Metabolic Studio, the New York City Department of Cultural Affairs in partnership with the City Council, the New York State Council on the Arts with the support of the Office of the Governor and the New York State Legislature, the Orbit Fund, the Robert Rauschenberg Foundation, the Stichting Egress Foundation, VIA Art Fund, The Jacques Louis Vidal Charitable Fund, Wagner Foundation, The Andy Warhol Foundation for the Visual Arts, the Wilhelm Family Foundation, and individuals worldwide. Primary Information receives support from the Arison Arts Foundation, The Willem de Kooning Foundation, the Marian Goodman Foundation, the Henry Luce Foundation, the Mellon Foundation, and Teiger Foundation through the Coalition of Small Arts NYC.